# CAKES
# & CAKE
# DECORATING

# CAKES
# & CAKE
# DECORATING

## ROSEMARY WADEY

# CONTENTS

## NOTE

1. All eggs are size 2 (large) unless otherwise stated.

2. All spoon measurements are level. Spoon measures can be bought in both imperial and metric sizes to give accurate measurement of small quantities.

3. Metric and imperial measurements have been calculated separately. Use one set of measurements only as they are not exact equivalents. In some recipes, you may find an apparent discrepancy in the metric equivalents. This is done to ensure a correct proportion of ingredients.

4. Cooking times may vary slightly depending on the individual oven. Dishes should be placed in the centre of the oven unless otherwise specified.

5. Always preheat the oven to the specified temperature.

6. Preparation times given are an average calculated during recipe testing.

**First published in 1982 by Octopus Books Limited**
**59 Grosvenor Street, London W1**

Seventh impression, 1984

© Hennerwood Publications Limited 1982

ISBN 0 906320 88 7

Produced by Mandarin Publishers Limited
22a Westlands Road, Quarry Bay, Hong Kong
Printed in Hong Kong

# INTRODUCTION

Decorating a cake can be fun and this fascinating book sets out to explain many of the secrets of successful cake icing and decorating, from the basic cake right through to the finished design, be it a simple sponge cake, a gâteau or an elaborately decorated celebration cake. Whether you are a beginner or more experienced, the step-by-step instructions will make all the techniques clear. Once you are familiar with the designs suggested, there's great scope for creating your own, too.

It is important, especially before starting a complicated decoration, to read right through the instructions carefully, then follow them step-by-step. In this way you will avoid finding yourself short of icing to complete the decoration!

Icing and intricate decorating take time, patience and skill for a perfect result. Therefore, it is a good idea to get lots of practice by beginning with the simple butter cream designs and the novelty cakes, which use many of the techniques required for the more complicated designs, and gradually to work up to the royal iced, celebration cakes. Because an evenly iced cake is an important basis for decoration a smooth royal icing finish can be practised on any type of basic cake. To get used to the special designs pipe them on any flat surface which can be wiped clean, ready for further attempts. Never work a design straight on to the cake for the first time; the result might ruin the cake and many hours of work already spent. If you don't have an icing turntable, an upturned cake tin provides a good edge necessary for border designs.

The separately made decorations, including models, run-outs and flowers, can be made up to 3–4 weeks in advance and this considerably reduces the last minute work involved in a complicated formal cake. Models are well worth the time and patience necessary, especially on the enchanting children's novelty cakes.

Altogether cake icing and decorating are rewarding skills, which can be enjoyed at any standard. Confidence is a great asset and there is no better way to gain this than to see your skills develop and the results improve.

# BASIC CAKE RECIPES

These are the general basic cakes which are used throughout the book, although some other cake recipes are included in later sections. In most recipes here the quantities are given in chart form which makes it easy to see how much mixture is required for a particular size of tin. Variations for flavours are also given.

The keeping qualities of the basic plain cakes vary and the following is a useful guide. The whisked sponge is best eaten on the day it is cooked or frozen for up to 2 months; the torten sponge cake should be eaten within 3 days, or it can be frozen for up to 1 month; the quick mix cake keeps well for 1 week; and the Madeira and Victoria sandwich cakes will keep for 7–10 days. These last three can be frozen for 1–2 months. If you don't intend freezing them, store the cakes in an airtight container, in a cool, dry atmosphere.

Because of the fairly short time that they are at their best the fruitless cakes are better coated with one of the less time-consuming, softer icings. However, once a cake has been iced it shouldn't be frozen. The exception to using one of the softer icings would be for a special occasion, when a Madeira cake could be covered with Marzipan (page 22), and Royal Icing (page 24) or the Gelatine or Moulding icing (pages 20 and 21).

A rich fruit cake is rather different because it improves with keeping. In particular, wedding cakes are best kept for 2–3 months before use. They should be kept in their greaseproof paper or wrapped in fresh greaseproof paper. Then, wrap them in foil and keep in a cool, dry atmosphere. As soon as the cake is cold, pierce all over with a fine skewer and pour brandy over (see individual recipes). This process can be repeated at monthly intervals to create a really rich and delicious fruit cake. If brandy or other spirits are added to the mixture before baking, much of the flavour is lost during the baking process; by adding it afterwards, both the flavour and alcoholic content are retained.

## LINING CAKE TINS

If using special non-stick tins, follow the manufacturer's instructions. With all other tins it is necessary either to grease and flour, or grease and line with greaseproof paper and grease again. Use oil, melted lard or melted margarine for greasing. If you wish to use non-stick silicone paper, there is no need to grease the paper.

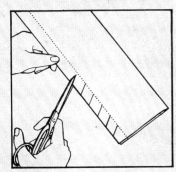

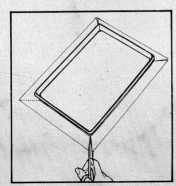

Above: For a round tin, make slanting cuts in the paper; Below: Insert strip

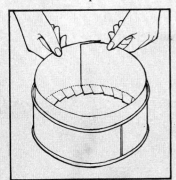

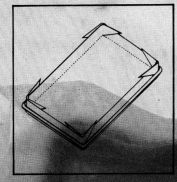

Above: For a shallow rectangular tin, make a cut from the corners; Below: Insert to fit neatly

## BASE LINING A ROUND OR SQUARE TIN

This method prevents the cake bottom falling out or sticking and is used for sponge and sandwich mixtures and lightly fruited cakes, but not for the rich cakes.
1.  Cut a single piece of greaseproof paper to fit the bottom of the tin.
2.  First grease the inside of the tin completely, then position the paper in the base and grease.

## TO DOUBLE LINE A DEEP ROUND TIN

For rich mixtures which require long cooking you should use double thickness of greaseproof paper and line both the sides and base of the tin. With the richer fruit cakes tie two or three thicknesses of brown paper or newspaper round the outside of the tin as an added protection against overcooking the outside of the cake.

For less rich mixtures follow the instructions below, using only single thickness greaseproof paper.
1.  Cut one or two strips of double greaseproof long enough to reach round the outside of the tin with enough to overlap, and wide enough to come 2.5 cm/ 1 inch above the rim of the tin. Fold the bottom edge up about 2 cm/¾ inch and crease it firmly. Open out and make slanting cuts into the folded strip at 2 cm/ ¾ inch intervals.
2.  Place the tin on a double thickness of greaseproof and draw round the base, then cut it out a little inside the line.
3.  Grease the inside of the tin, place one paper circle in the base and grease just round the edge of the paper.
4.  Place the long strips in the tin, pressing them against the sides with the cut edges spread over the base. Grease all over the side paper.
5.  Finally position the second circle in the base and grease again.

## TO DOUBLE LINE A DEEP SQUARE OR RECTANGULAR TIN

Follow the instructions for the deep round tin but make folds into the corners of the long strips.

## TO LINE A SHALLOW RECTANGULAR TIN

For Swiss rolls and similar cakes it is always wise to line and grease for easy removal.
1.  Cut a piece of greaseproof about 7.5 cm/ 3 inches larger than the tin (and larger still if the sides of the tin are deeper than 2.5 cm/1 inch).
2.  Place the tin on the paper and make a cut from the corners of the paper to the corners of the tin.
3.  Grease inside the tin, put in the paper so that it fits neatly, overlapping the paper at the corners to give sharp angles, and grease again.

## TO LINE A LOAF TIN

Use the same method as for lining a shallow rectangular tin but cut the paper at least 15 cm/6 inches larger than the top of the tin. Grease the tin, position the paper, fitting the corners neatly, and grease again.

## WASHING DRIED FRUIT

Most packaged dried fruit is pre-washed and needs no further attention, although it may be a good idea to look it over, for the odd stalk can sometimes slip through. Dried fruit bought loose may require rinsing in cold water and thorough drying before use. Excess moisture can be removed with paper towels or clean cloths and the fruit should then be spread out on baking sheets covered with paper towels or clean cloths and left in a fairly warm (not hot) place to dry. This will take up to 24 hours and fruit should be moved round once or twice during this time. Never use wet fruit in cakes, as it will sink immediately.

## RICH FRUIT CAKE INGREDIENTS

| | | | | | | | | |
|---|---|---|---|---|---|---|---|---|
| SQUARE | 13 cm/ 5 inch | 15 cm/ 6 inch | 18 cm/ 7 inch | 20 cm/ 8 inch | 23 cm/ 9 inch | 25 cm/ 10 inch | 28 cm/ 11 inch | 30 cm/ 12 inch |
| ROUND | 15 cm/ 6 inch | 18 cm/ 7 inch | 20 cm/ 8 inch | 23 cm/ 9 inch | 25 cm/ 10 inch | 28 cm/ 11 inch | 30 cm/ 12 inch | |
| SLAB CAKE | | | | 29 × 21 × 4 cm/ 11½ × 8½ × 1½ inch | 30 × 25 × 5 cm/ 12 × 10 × 2 inch | | | |
| currants | 150 g/ 5 oz | 225 g/ 8 oz | 350 g/ 12 oz | 450 g/ 1 lb | 625 g/ 1 lb 6 oz | 775 g/ 1 lb 12 oz | 1.2 kg/ 2 lb 8 oz | 1.4 kg/ 3 lb |
| sultanas | 50 g/ 2 oz | 90 g/ 3½ oz | 125 g/ 4½ oz | 200 g/ 7 oz | 225 g/ 8 oz | 375 g/ 13 oz | 400 g/ 14 oz | 500 g/ 1 lb 2 oz |
| raisins | 50 g/ 2 oz | 90 g/ 3½ oz | 125 g/ 4½ oz | 200 g/ 7 oz | 225 g/ 8 oz | 375 g/ 13 oz | 400 g/ 14 oz | 500 g/ 1 lb 2 oz |
| glacé cherries | 40 g/ 1½ oz | 65 g/ 2½ oz | 75 g/ 3 oz | 100 g/ 4 oz | 150 g/ 5 oz | 225 g/ 8 oz | 300 g/ 10 oz | 350 g/ 12 oz |
| mixed peel, chopped | 25 g/ 1 oz | 50 g/ 2 oz | 50 g/ 2 oz | 75 g/ 3 oz | 100 g/ 4 oz | 150 g/ 5 oz | 200 g/ 7 oz | 250 g/ 9 oz |
| blanched almonds, chopped | 25 g/ 1 oz | 50 g/ 2 oz | 50 g/ 2 oz | 75 g/ 3 oz | 100 g/ 4 oz | 150 g/ 5 oz | 200 g/ 7 oz | 250 g/ 9 oz |
| lemon rind, grated | ¼ lemon | ½ lemon | ¾ lemon | 1 lemon | 1 lemon | 1 lemon | 1½ lemons | 2 lemons |
| plain flour | 100 g/ 3½ oz | 175 g/ 6 oz | 200 g/ 7½ oz | 350 g/ 12 oz | 400 g/ 14 oz | 600 g/ 1 lb 5 oz | 700 g/ 1 lb 8 oz | 825 g/ 1 lb 13 oz |
| ground cinnamon | ½ teaspoon | ½ teapoon | ¾ teaspoon | 1 teaspoon | 1½ teaspoons | 2 teaspoons | 2½ teaspoons | 2¾ teaspoons |
| ground mixed spice | ¼ teaspoon | ¼ teaspoon | ½ teaspoon | ¾ teaspoon | 1 teaspoon | 1¼ teaspoons | 1½ teaspoons | 1¾ teaspoons |
| butter | 75 g/ 3 oz | 150 g/ 5 oz | 175 g/ 6 oz | 275 g/ 10 oz | 350 g/ 12 oz | 500 g/ 1 lb 2 oz | 600 g/ 1 lb 5 oz | 800 g/ 1 lb 12 oz |
| soft brown sugar | 75 g/ 3 oz | 150 g/ 5 oz | 175 g/ 6 oz | 275 g/ 10 oz | 350 g/ 12 oz | 500 g/ 1 lb 2 oz | 600 g/ 1 lb 5 oz | 800 g/ 1 lb 12 oz |
| eggs (size 2) | 1½ | 2½ | 3 | 5 | 6 | 9 | 11 | 14 |
| black treacle (optional) | 1 teaspoon | 1 teaspoon | 1 tablespoon | 1 tablespoon | 1 tablespoon | 2 tablespoons | 2 tablespoons | 2 tablespoons |
| *Approx cooking time* | *2 hours* | *2½ hours* | *2¾ hours* | *3¼ hours* | *3¾ hours* | *4¼–4½ hours* | *5¼–5½ hours* | *6–6½ hours* |
| *Approx cooked weight* | *750 g/ 1½ lb* | *1.25 kg/ 2½ lb* | *1.5 kg/ 3¼ lb* | *2 kg/ 4½ lb* | *2.75 kg/ 6 lb* | *4 kg/ 9 lb* | *5 kg/ 11 lb* | *6.5 kg/ 14 lb* |
| brandy, added after cooking | 2 tablespoons | 3 tablespoons | 3 tablespoons | 4 tablespoons | 5 tablespoons | 6 tablespoons | 7 tablespoons | 8 tablespoons |

# RICH FRUIT CAKE

*Preparation time: about 25 minutes,
    plus maturing*
*Cooking time: see chart*
*Oven: 150°C, 300°F, Gas Mark 2*

This fruit cake improves with keeping and makes a delicious Christmas cake. For the smaller cakes, especially the top tiers of a wedding cake, it is often a good idea to add a little gravy browning to the mixture so it will be the same dark colour as the larger cakes which tend to go darker.

1.  Mix together the currants, sultanas and raisins.
2.  Cut the glacé cherries into quarters, rinse under warm water and dry thoroughly on kitchen paper.
3.  Add the cherries to the dried fruit mixture with the mixed peel, almonds and grated lemon rind. Mix well.
4.  Sift the flour, ground cinnamon and mixed spice together.
5.  Cream the butter until soft, then add the sugar and continue creaming until light and fluffy. Do not overbeat or the cake will become coarse in texture and heavy.
6.  Add the eggs to the creamed mixture one at a time, beating in well and following each with a spoonful of flour.
7.  Fold in the remaining flour, followed by the dried fruit mixture.
8.  Add the black treacle, if using.

9.  Spread the mixture evenly in a greased and double-lined tin(s) (see page 9). Using the back of a spoon make a slight hollow in the centre so that the top of the cake comes out flat.
10.  Tie two or three thicknesses of brown paper or newspaper round the tin, then place in a preheated oven. Bake for the time suggested in the chart. If the cake seems to be overbrowning, lay a sheet of greaseproof paper lightly over the top. With very large cakes, it is sometimes better to turn the oven down to 140°C, 275°F, Gas Mark 1 after about two-thirds of the cooking time has been completed.
11.  To test if the cake is done insert a skewer into the centre: it should come out clean. Remove from the oven and leave to cool in the tin. Turn on to a wire rack and remove the lining paper.
12.  Prick the top of the cake all over with a skewer, then spoon several tablespoons of brandy or other spirit over the top. Wrap in greaseproof paper and foil, and store. If possible, repeat this process at monthly intervals while maturing. This cake should be allowed to mature for 2–3 months.

## QUICK MIX CAKE INGREDIENTS

| CAKE SIZES | 2 × 18 cm/ 7 inch sandwich tins | 18 paper cake cases or patty tins | 20 cm/8 inch sandwich tin<br><br>20 cm/8 inch ring mould<br><br>18 cm/ 7 inch deep square tin | *900 ml/ 1½ pint pudding basin | about 26 paper cake cases or patty tins | 2 × 20 cm/ 8 inch sandwich tins | 23 cm/ 9 inch sandwich tin |
|---|---|---|---|---|---|---|---|
| soft (tub) margarine, chilled | 100 g/4 oz | 100 g/4 oz | 100 g/4 oz | 100 g/4 oz | 175 g/6 oz | 175 g/6 oz | 175 g/6 oz |
| caster sugar | 100 g/4 oz | 100 g/4 oz | 100 g/4 oz | 100 g/4 oz | 175 g/6 oz | 175 g/6 oz | 175 g/6 oz |
| eggs (sizes 1, 2) | 2 | 2 | 2 | 2 | 3 | 3 | 3 |
| self-raising flour | 100 g/4 oz | 100 g/4 oz | 100 g/4 oz | 100 g/4 oz | 175 g/6 oz | 175 g/6 oz | 175 g/6 oz |
| baking power | 1 teaspoon | 1 teaspoon | 1 teaspoon | 1 teaspoon | 1½ teaspoons | 1½ teaspoons | 1½ teaspoons |
| vanilla essence | 4 drops | 4 drops | 4 drops | 4 drops | 6 drops | 6 drops | 6 drops |
| *Approx. cooking time* | *25–30 minutes* | *15–20 minutes* | *35–40 minutes* | *about 50 minutes* | *15–20 minutes* | *30–35 minutes* | *about 25 minutes* |

| CAKE SIZES | 28 × 18 × 4 cm/ 11 × 7 × 1½ inch slab cake<br><br>20 cm/8 inch round tin<br><br>20 cm/8 inch square tin | *1 litre/ 2 pint pudding basin | 29 × 21 × 4 cm/ 11½ × 8½ × 1½ inch slab cake | 23 cm/9 inch round tin<br><br>23 cm/9 inch square tin | 30 × 25 × 5 cm/ 12 × 10 × 2 inch slab cake |
|---|---|---|---|---|---|
| soft (tub) margarine, chilled | 175 g/6 oz | 175 g/6 oz | 200 g/8 oz | 200 g/8 oz | 275 g/10 oz |
| caster sugar | 175 g/6 oz | 175 g/6 oz | 200 g/8 oz | 200 g/8 oz | 275 g/10 oz |
| eggs (sizes 1, 2) | 3 | 3 | 4 | 4 | 5 |
| self-raising flour | 175 g/6 oz | 175 g/6 oz | 200 g/8 oz | 200 g/8 oz | 275 g/10 oz |
| baking powder | 1½ teaspoons | 1½ teaspoons | 2 teaspoons | 2 teaspoons | 2½ teaspoons |
| vanilla essence | 6 drops | 6 drops | 8 drops | 8 drops | 10 drops |
| *Approx. cooking time* | *35–40 minutes* | *about 1 hour* | *about 40 minutes* | *about 1 hour* | *about 50–60 minutes* |

*add 25 g/1 oz cornflour sifted with the flour.

# QUICK MIX CAKE

*Preparation time: about 5 minutes*
*Cooking time: see chart*
*Oven: 160°C, 325°F, Gas Mark 3*

1. Put the margarine, sugar, eggs, sifted flour and baking powder, and vanilla essence into a bowl.
2. Mix together with a wooden spoon or hand-held electric mixer, then beat hard for 1–2 minutes until smooth and glossy.
3. Turn into a greased and floured tin(s), level the top and bake in a preheated oven for the time suggested in the chart or until well-risen, just firm to the touch and the sides of the cake are beginning to shrink from the sides of the tin.
4. Loosen the sides of the cake from the tin and turn on to a wire rack. Invert the cake on to another wire rack, unless baked in a ring mould or basin. Leave to cool.

**VARIATIONS:**
*Chocolate Quick Mix Cake:* omit the vanilla essence and add 1 tablespoon sifted cocoa powder for the 2-egg mixture, 1½ tablespoons for the 3-egg mixture, 2 tablespoons for the 4-egg mixture, and 2½ tablespoons for the 5-egg mixture.
*Coffee Quick Mix Cake:* omit the vanilla essence and add 2 teaspoons instant coffee powder or 1 tablespoon coffee essence for the 2-egg mixture, 3 teaspoons coffee powder or 1½ tablespoons coffee essence for the 3-egg mixture, 4 teaspoons coffee powder or 2 tablespoons coffee essence for the 4-egg mixture, and 5 teaspoons coffee powder or 2½ tablespoons coffee essence for the 5-egg mixture.
*Orange or Lemon Quick Mix Cake:* omit the vanilla and add 2 teaspoons finely grated orange or lemon rind for the 2-egg mixture, 3 teaspoons orange or lemon rind for the 3-egg mixture, 4 teaspoons orange or lemon rind for the 4-egg mixture and 5 teaspoons orange or lemon rind for the 5-egg mixture.

# WHISKED SPONGE CAKE

| CAKE SIZES | 2 × 18 cm/ 7 inch sandwich tins | 20 cm/8 inch sandwich tin<br><br>18 cm/7 inch square tin | 28 × 18 cm/ 11 × 7 inch Swiss roll tin | 18 sponge drops | 20 cm/8 inch round cake tin | 2 × 20 cm/ 8 inch sandwich tins | 28 × 18 × 4 cm/ 11 × 7 × 1½ inch slab cake | 30 × 23 cm/ 12 × 9 inch Swiss roll tin |
|---|---|---|---|---|---|---|---|---|
| eggs (sizes 1, 2) | 2 | 2 | 2 | 2 | 3 | 3 | 3 | 3 |
| caster sugar | 50 g/2 oz | 50 g/2 oz | 50 g/2 oz | 50 g/2 oz | 75 g/3 oz | 75 g/3 oz | 75 g/3 oz | 75 g/3 oz |
| plain flour | 50 g/2 oz | 50 g/2 oz | 50 g/2 oz | 50 g/2 oz | 75 g/3 oz | 75 g/3 oz | 75 g/3 oz | 75 g/3 oz |
| baking power | ½ teaspoon | ½ teaspoon | ½ teaspoon | ½ teaspoon | ½ teaspoon | ½ teaspoon | ½ teaspoon | ½ teaspoon |
| *Approx. cooking time* | 20–25 minutes | 25–30 minutes | 10–12 minutes | 5–10 minutes | 35–40 minutes | 20–25 minutes | 30–35 minutes | 12–15 minutes |
| *Oven* | 180°C, 350°F, Gas Mark 4 | 180°C, 350°F, Gas Mark 4 | 190°C, 375°F, Gas Mark 5 | 190°C, 375°F, Gas Mark 5 | 180°C, 350°F, Gas Mark 4 | 180°C, 350°F, Gas Mark 4 | 180°C, 350°F, Gas Mark 4 | 200°C, 400°F, Gas Mark 6 |

*Preparation time: 10–15 minutes*
*Cooking time: see chart*
*Oven: see chart*

1. Put the eggs and sugar in a heatproof bowl over a saucepan of hot but not boiling water. Whisk until the mixture becomes very thick and pale in colour and the whisk leaves a heavy trail when lifted. Remove the bowl from the saucepan and continue whisking until the cake mixture is cool.
2. Alternatively, the whisking may be done with an electric mixer, without heat.
3. Sift the flour and baking powder together, then sift again over the whisked mixture. Using a metal spoon, fold in the flour quickly and evenly.
4. Turn into a greased and single-lined tin(s) (page 9) and shake gently or spread lightly with a palette knife until level. Bake in a preheated oven for the time suggested in the chart or until the cake springs back when gently pressed with the fingertips and has begun to shrink a little from the sides of the tin.

5. Turn on to a wire rack and remove the lining paper. Leave to cool.
6. If making a Swiss roll, invert the cake on to a sheet of greaseproof paper sprinkled liberally with caster sugar. Quickly peel off the lining paper and trim the edges of the cake with a sharp knife. Fold the top short edge of the cake in about 2.5 cm/1 inch, then roll up the cake loosely with the paper inside. (This process must be completed immediately the cake is taken out of the oven for it will not roll up without cracking if it is allowed to cool any more than necessary.) Leave to cool and set for a few minutes, then carefully unroll and remove the paper. Fill with jam, butter cream, or fruit and whipped cream, and roll up again.

**VARIATIONS:**
*Lemon or Orange Whisked Sponge Cake:* add the grated rind of ½ lemon or orange with the flour.
*Chocolate Whisked Sponge Cake:* replace 15 g/ ½ oz of the flour with sifted cocoa powder.
*Coffee Whisked Sponge Cake:* add 2 teaspoons instant coffee powder with the flour.

# TORTEN SPONGE CAKE

*Preparation time: about 20 minutes*
*Cooking time: 30 minutes for a deep round cake or 20 minutes for a rectangular cake*
*Oven: 190°C, 375°F, Gas Mark 5*

50 g/2 oz butter
75 g/3 oz self-raising flour
3 eggs (sizes 1, 2)
100 g/4 oz caster sugar

If you find it difficult cutting through a cake, this sponge can be baked in two 20 cm/8 inch greased and lined sandwich tins, allowing about 20 minutes' cooking time.

1.  Grease and single line a deep 20 cm/8 inch round cake tin or a 28 × 18 × 4 cm/11 × 7 × 1½ inch rectangular tin (see page 9).
2.  Heat the butter gently until just melted, remove from the heat and leave to stand so the sediment sinks to the bottom.
3.  Sift the flour twice.
4.  Place the eggs and sugar in a large heatproof bowl and stand over a pan of gently simmering water. Whisk until light and creamy, and thick enough for the whisk to leave a heavy trail when lifted. Remove from the heat and continue to whisk until cool. If using an electric mixer it is not necessary to stand the bowl over hot water.
5.  Fold the sifted flour lightly and evenly through the mixture.

**Left: Whisked sponge Swiss roll**
**Below: Plain and chocolate torten sponge cakes**

6.  Carefully pour in the butter, without the sediment, and fold in carefully and lightly.
7.  Turn into the prepared tin and bake in a preheated oven for about 30 minutes for a round cake or 20 minutes for a rectangular cake, or until well risen, golden brown and firm to the touch. Turn out and cool on a wire rack. Remove the lining paper.

**VARIATIONS:**
*Chocolate Torten Sponge Cake:* replace 15 g/½ oz of the flour with sifted cocoa powder.
*Lemon or Orange Torten Sponge Cake:* add the very finely grated rind of 1 small lemon or ½ orange to the eggs and sugar before whisking.
*Coffee Torten Sponge Cake:* replace 2 level teaspoons of the flour with instant coffee powder.

# MADEIRA CAKE

*Preparation time: about 15 minutes*
*Cooking time: see chart*
*Oven: 160°C, 325°F, Gas Mark 3*

Madeira cake can be covered with marzipan and royal or other icing. The lemon rind and juice may be replaced with orange.

1. Cream the butter and sugar together until light and fluffy, and very pale in colour.
2. Beat in the eggs one at a time, following each with a spoonful of flour.
3. Sift the rest of the flours together and fold into the creamed mixture followed by the lemon rind and juice.
4. Turn into a greased and single lined tin (see page 9) and level the top.
5. Bake in a preheated oven for the time suggested in the chart or until well risen, firm to the touch and golden brown.
6. Cool in the tin for 5–10 minutes. Turn on to a wire rack to cool, then remove the lining paper.

| CAKE SIZES | 15 cm/6 inch round or square tin | 18 cm/7 inch round tin | *18 cm/7 inch round tin 900 g/2 lb loaf tin | 18 cm/7 inch square tin | 20 cm/8 inch round tin | *20 cm/8 inch round tin | 20 cm/8 inch square tin |
|---|---|---|---|---|---|---|---|
| butter | 100 g/4 oz | 100 g/4 oz | 150 g/6 oz | 150 g/6 oz | 150 g/6 oz | 200 g/8 oz | 200 g/8 oz |
| caster sugar | 100 g/4 oz | 100 g/4 oz | 150 g/6 oz | 150 g/6 oz | 150 g/6 oz | 200 g/8 oz | 200 g/8 oz |
| eggs (sizes 1, 2) | 2 | 2 | 3 | 3 | 3 | 4 | 4 |
| self-raising flour | 100 g/4 oz | 100 g/4 oz | 150 g/6 oz | 150 g/6 oz | 150 g/6 oz | 200 g/8 oz | 200 g/8 oz |
| plain flour | 50 g/2 oz | 50 g/2 oz | 75 g/3 oz | 75 g/3 oz | 75 g/3 oz | 100 g/4 oz | 100 g/4 oz |
| grated lemon rind | ½–1 lemon | ½–1 lemon | 1 lemon | 1 lemon | 1 lemon | 1½ lemons | 1½ lemons |
| lemon juice | 2 teaspoons | 2 teaspoons | 1 tablespoon | 1 tablespoon | 1 tablespoon | 4 teaspoons | 4 teaspoons |
| *Approx cooking time* | *1 hour* | *50 minutes* | *1¼ hours* | *1 hour 5–10 minutes* | *1 hour* | *1 hour 20–25 minutes* | *1 hour 15–20 minutes* |

| CAKE SIZES | 23 cm/9 inch round tin | 28 × 18 × 4 cm/ 11 × 7 × 1½ inch slab cake | *23 cm/9 inch round tin | 23 cm/9 inch square tin | 25 cm/10 inch round tin | 30 × 25 × 5 cm/ 12 × 10 × 2 inch slab cake |
|---|---|---|---|---|---|---|
| butter | 200 g/8 oz | 200 g/8 oz | 250 g/10 oz | 250 g/10 oz | 250 g/10 oz | 250 g/10 oz |
| caster sugar | 200 g/8 oz | 200 g/8 oz | 250 g/10 oz | 250 g/10 oz | 250 g/10 oz | 250 g/10 oz |
| eggs (sizes 1, 2) | 4 | 4 | 5 | 5 | 5 | 5 |
| self-raising flour | 200 g/8 oz | 200 g/8 oz | 250 g/10 oz | 250 g/10 oz | 250 g/10 oz | 250 g/10 oz |
| plain flour | 100 g/4 oz | 100 g/4 oz | 125 g/5 oz | 125 g/5 oz | 125 g/5 oz | 125 g/5 oz |
| grated lemon rind | 1½ lemons | 1½ lemons | 2 lemons | 2 lemons | 2 lemons | 2 lemons |
| lemon juice | 4 teaspoons | 4 teaspoons | 2 tablespoons | 2 tablespoons | 2 tablespoons | 2 tablespoons |
| *Approx cooking time* | *1 hour 10 minutes* | *1–1¼ hours* | *1 hour 30–40 minutes* | *1 hour 25–30 minutes* | *1 hour 20 minutes* | *1 hour 15–20 minutes* |

*These quantities make a deeper cake

# VICTORIA SPONGE CAKE

*Preparation time: about 30 minutes*
*Cooking time: 20–25 minutes*
*Oven: 190°C, 375°F, Gas Mark 5*

150 g/6 oz caster sugar
150 g/6 oz butter or soft margarine
3 eggs (sizes 1, 2)
150 g/6 oz self-raising flour
1 tablespoon water

1. Cream the sugar and butter or margarine together until light and fluffy, and pale in colour.
2. Beat in the eggs one at a time following each with a spoonful of the flour.
3. Sift the remaining flour and fold into the creamed mixture alternately with the water.
4. Divide the cake mixture between two greased and floured 20 cm/8 inch round sandwich tins or fill a 28 × 18 × 4 cm/ 11 × 7 × 1½ inch rectangular cake tin. Level the surface and bake in a preheated oven for 20–25 minutes or until well risen and firm to the touch. Turn on to a wire rack to cool.

**VARIATIONS:**
*Chocolate Victoria Sponge Cake:* replace 25 g/ 1 oz of the flour with 25 g/1 oz sifted cocoa powder. Add with the remaining flour.
*Coffee Victoria Sponge Cake:* replace the water with coffee essence or dissolve 2 teaspoons instant coffee powder in 1 tablespoon boiling water.
*Lemon or Orange Victoria Sponge Cake:* add the very finely grated rind of 1 lemon or orange.

**Victoria sponge cake filled with jam; Madeira cake; Victoria and Madeira cake mixtures**

# ICINGS, FROSTINGS & FILLINGS

How do you cover a cake with marzipan? How long does it need to dry before adding the icing? My royal icing never goes smooth – why? These questions and many more are fully answered in this chapter with clear instructions and photographs to help you perfect your decorated cakes.

The icings range from rich butter creams and frostings to traditional royal icing and the less known moulding and gelatine icings which are ideal for both covering cakes and making decorations. All these icings and fillings are featured in the cakes throughout the book.

**From the left: American frosting; Butterscotch seven minute frosting; Chocolate icing**

The soft icings and frostings can be used for any of the cakes, except the rich fruit varieties. They should be spread straight on to the cake; or if the cake is the type with a lot of loose crumbs, it can be covered first with a layer of apricot glaze as a base for the icing. A thin layer of marzipan can also be used under any of the icings or frostings. This will help to smooth glacé icing, in particular. A fruit cake must have a layer of marzipan before being iced.

Royal icing is generally used for fruit cakes and is always spread over a layer of marzipan. Only royal icing can be used for tiered wedding cakes as no other type dries firmly enough to take the weight. It can also be used on sponge and Madeira cakes, but remember these cakes do not keep for very long (see page 8). Moulding and gelatine icing can be put straight on to fruitless cakes after brushing first with apricot glaze, but a better finish is achieved with a layer of marzipan.

# AMERICAN FROSTING

*Preparation time: 20–30 minutes*
*Makes sufficient to fill and cover a*
*20–23 cm/8–9 inch cake*

450 g/1 lb loaf or granulated sugar
150 ml/¼ pint water
pinch of cream of tartar
2 egg whites
food colouring (optional)

Suitable for most cakes, this frosting has a crisp outer crust with a soft inside. To guarantee success a sugar thermometer must be used, and it is vital to beat until the frosting really does stand in peaks or it may slide off the cake.

1. Put the sugar and water into a large heavy-based saucepan and heat gently until the sugar has dissolved. Add the cream of tartar.
2. Insert a sugar thermometer and bring to the boil. Boil to a temperature of 115°C/240°F.
3. Meanwhile, beat the egg whites until very stiff.
4. Pour the sugar syrup in a thin stream on to the beaten egg whites, beating briskly all the time. Continue to beat until the frosting is thick enough to stand in peaks with the tips just tipping over. Add food colouring while beating, if using.
5. Quickly spread the frosting over the cake, pulling it into peaks all over the cake. Leave to set.

**VARIATIONS:**
*Coffee Frosting:* add 1 teaspoon coffee essence to the mixture while beating.
*Chocolate Frosting:* add 1–2 teaspoons cocoa powder dissolved in 1 teaspoon warm water while beating.

# SEVEN MINUTE FROSTING

*Preparation time: 7–10 minutes*
*Makes sufficient to fill and cover an*
*18 cm/7 inch sandwich cake*

1 egg white
150 g/6 oz caster sugar
pinch of salt
2 tablespoons water
pinch of cream of tartar

This is a much quicker version of the traditional American Frosting (above), which does not require a sugar thermometer. It must be used immediately as it sets very quickly.

1. Put all the ingredients into a heatproof bowl and mix lightly.
2. Place over a saucepan of gently simmering water and beat hard, if possible with a hand-held electric mixer, until the mixture is thick and stiff enough to stand in peaks.
3. Remove from the heat and pour over the cake. Spread the frosting at once to cover all over and pull up into peaks.
4. Leave to set.

**VARIATION:**
*Butterscotch Frosting:* use sifted light soft brown sugar in place of caster sugar.

# CHOCOLATE ICING

*Preparation time: about 10 minutes*
*Makes sufficient to fill and cover a*
*20 cm/8 inch sandwich cake*

100 g/4 oz plain chocolate, broken
into pieces
50 g/2 oz butter
2 egg yolks
about 100 g/4 oz icing sugar, sifted

This is a type of chocolate fudge icing; for a smoother finish to the icing add less icing sugar.

1. Put the chocolate and butter in the top of a double saucepan or heatproof bowl over a pan of gently simmering water.
2. Heat until the chocolate melts, then remove from the heat and beat until smooth.
3. Beat in the egg yolks and sufficient sugar to give a thick, smooth, spreading consistency.
4. Cool slightly so the icing will not run off the edge of the cake. When spread over the top and sides of a cake, swirl it into peaks with a palette knife. Leave to set.

# GLACE ICING

*Makes sufficient to cover the top of a
20 cm/8 inch round cake*
*Preparation time: about 5 minutes*

225 g/8 oz icing sugar
2–4 tablespoons hot water
food colouring and/or flavouring
(optional)

This is the quickest of icings to make and useful for icing sponge, sandwich and other cakes, as well as small cakes and biscuits. The icing will remain liquid if the bowl is placed in another larger bowl containing hot water.

1.  Sift the icing sugar into a bowl.
2.  Gradually beat in sufficient water to give a smooth icing, thick enough to coat the back of the spoon. Extra water or sugar can be added to achieve the correct consistency.
3.  Add a few drops of food colouring or flavouring, if using. Use at once or place over hot water for a short period.
4.  Alternatively, put all the ingredients into a saucepan and heat gently, stirring, until well mixed and smooth; take care not to overheat or the icing will crystallize.

**VARIATIONS:**
*Lemon or Orange Glacé Icing:* use strained fruit juice instead of water. A few drops of food colouring can also be added.
*Coffee Glacé Icing:* use a little coffee essence or strong black coffee in place of part of the water.
*Chocolate Glacé Icing:* dissolve 2 teaspoons cocoa powder in the water and add to the icing sugar.
*Mocha Glacé Icing:* dissolve 1 teaspoon cocoa powder and 2 teaspoons instant coffee powder in the water and add to the icing sugar.

# GELATINE ICING

*Makes sufficient to cover a 20 cm/
8 inch round cake*
*Preparation time: about 10 minutes*

2 teaspoons powdered gelatine
2 tablespoons water
about 550 g/1¼ lb icing sugar
1 egg white
1 teaspoon glycerine
food colouring (optional)

This icing can be used to cover the top and sides of a cake, and for cut out or moulded decorations. It is interchangeable with Moulding Icing (see right).

1.  Put the gelatine and water in a heatproof bowl. Place over a saucepan of hot but not boiling water and dissolve the gelatine, stirring occasionally. Remove from the heat and allow to cool.
2.  Sift the icing sugar into another bowl. Add the dissolved gelatine, egg white and glycerine.
3.  Mix together with a wooden spoon to form a dough, then knead until smooth, adding extra icing sugar if necessary. Add the food colouring, if using, by kneading it into the icing.
4.  The icing can be stored in an airtight container or tightly-sealed polythene bag in a cool place for 2–3 days before use. If the icing begins to dry out on the surface, dip the container briefly in hot water, leave for 1 hour, then knead well again before using.

# MOULDING ICING

*Makes sufficient to cover a 20 cm/
8 inch round cake*
*Preparation time: 10–15 minutes*

450 g/1 lb icing sugar
1 egg white
50 g/2 oz liquid glucose
food colouring and/or flavouring
(optional)

Also known as kneaded fondant icing and interchangeable with Gelatine Icing (see left), this is simple to use once you get used to its consistency. Use it for modelling all types of animals, figures, flowers, etc., either by colouring the icing first or by painting with liquid food colourings when completed. It is also suitable for covering all types of cakes except tiered wedding cakes – it will not set firm enough to take the weight of the other tiers.

Liquid glucose or glucose syrup is available from chemist shops.

1. Sift the icing sugar into a mixing bowl and make a well in the centre.
2. Add the egg white and liquid glucose. Beat with a wooden spoon, gradually pulling in the icing sugar from the sides of the bowl, to give a stiff mixture.
3. Knead the icing thoroughly, mixing in any remaining icing sugar in the bowl to give a smooth and manageable paste.
4. Add colouring and flavouring as desired and extra sifted icing sugar, if necessary.
5. The icing can be stored in a tightly-sealed polythene bag or a plastic container in a cool place for 2–3 days before use.

## HOW TO APPLY MOULDING OR GELATINE ICING TO A CAKE

Attach moulding or gelatine icing to a cake covered with Marzipan (page 22) after brushing the marzipan with egg white, or to a cake without marzipan after brushing with Apricot Glaze (page 27).

1. Roll out the icing on a surface dredged with icing sugar, or between two sheets of polythene, to a round or square about 10 cm/4 inches larger than the cake top.
2. Support the icing on a rolling pin and place over the top of the cake.
3. Press the icing on to the sides of the cake, working the icing evenly to the back of the cake. Dip your hands in cornflour and/or icing sugar and rub the surface in a circular movement to give an even covering. Cut off excess icing.
4. For square cakes cut out a piece of icing at each corner and mould carefully to give even-shaped corners. Leave to dry.

**Left: Applying gelatine or moulding icing; Below: Glacé icing setting inside non-stick silicone paper**

# MARZIPAN OR ALMOND PASTE

*Makes 450 g/1 lb*
*Preparation time: about 10 minutes*

100 g/4 oz caster sugar
100 g/4 oz icing sugar, sifted
200 g/8 oz ground almonds
1 teaspoon lemon juice
few drops of almond essence
1 egg or 2 egg yolks, beaten

This is used for covering all cakes to be coated with royal icing, for decorative tops to cakes, or for moulding animals, flowers, leaves, etc., for decoration. It can be coloured with liquid, powder or paste food colouring. For a white marzipan use two egg whites instead of an egg or egg yolks.

1.  Combine the sugars and ground almonds and make a well in the centre.
2.  Add the lemon juice, almond essence and sufficient egg or egg yolks to mix to a firm but manageable dough.
3.  Turn on to a lightly sugared surface and knead until smooth. The marzipan can be wrapped in polythene or foil and stored for 2–3 days before use.

## HOW TO APPLY MARZIPAN TO A CAKE

*Approximate quantities of marzipan for square and round cakes*

| SQUARE | | 15 cm/6 inch | 18 cm/7 inch | 20 cm/8 inch | 23 cm/9 inch | 25 cm/10 inch | 28 cm/11 inch | 30 cm/12 inch |
|---|---|---|---|---|---|---|---|---|
| ROUND | 15 cm/6 inch | 18 cm/7 inch | 20 cm/8 inch | 23 cm/9 inch | 25 cm/10 inch | 28 cm/11 inch | 30 cm/12 inch | |
| *Marzipan* | 350 g/¾ lb | 450 g/1 lb | 575 g/1¼ lb | 800 g/1¾ lb | 900 g/2 lb | 1 kg/2¼ lb | 1.25 kg/2½ lb | 1.4 kg/3 lb |

The same method is used for both round and square cakes. Make up the required quantity of marzipan for the cake, or use a commercial marzipan.

1.  Place almost half of the marzipan on a working surface dredged with icing sugar, or between two sheets of polythene. Roll out evenly until 2.5 cm/1 inch larger than the top of the cake.
2.  Brush the top of the cake with Apricot Glaze (page 27). Invert the cake on to the marzipan. Using a small palette knife, draw up the edge of the marzipan, attaching it to the sides of the cake and giving an even edge to the top of the cake.
3.  Place the cake, marzipan-side up, on a cake board and brush the sides with apricot glaze.
4.  Cut two pieces of string, one the exact height of the cake and the other the complete circumference. Roll out the remaining marzipan to a strip the circumference and height of the cake, or in two shorter strips if easier.
5.  Loosely roll the marzipan strip into a coil. Place one end on the side of the cake and unroll carefully, moulding the marzipan to the side of the cake and making sure the marzipan touches the board.

6.  Using a small palette knife, smooth the join at the ends of the strip and where the strip meets the marzipan on top of the cake. If the marzipan seems unduly moist, rub all over with sifted icing sugar.
7.  Store the cake, uncovered, in a warm dry place for at least 24 hours before applying any icing. For tiered wedding cakes the marzipan should be allowed to dry in the same way for at least a week before icing to prevent the oils from the marzipan seeping into the royal icing during storage after the wedding.

# ROYAL ICING

*Preparation time: about 15 minutes*

3 egg whites
about 675 g/1½ lb icing sugar, sifted
2–3 teaspoons strained lemon juice
1–1½ teaspoons glycerine (optional)

Royal icing can be made in any quantity as long as you allow 1 egg white to each 225 g/8 oz icing sugar. However, it is better to make up not more than a 900 g/2 lb quantity of icing at a time because the icing keeps better if made in small quantities. While using the icing, cover the bowl with a damp cloth to prevent a skin forming. Powdered egg albumen, which is available from specialist cake shops, can be made up according to the instructions on the packet and used in place of fresh egg whites.

Glycerine can be added to help soften the icing and make cutting easier. It should be omitted from the icing for the first couple of coats on the top surface of the bottom tier of a wedding cake and the first coat on the top surface of the middle tier, because a hard surface is needed to take the weight of the other tiers.

The icing can be stored in an airtight container in a cool room for up to 2 days. It should, however, be stirred very thoroughly before use.

1. Beat the egg whites until frothy, then gradually beat in half the sugar using a wooden spoon. A mixer can be used but it will incorporate a lot of air and the resulting bubbles will be difficult to disperse.
2. Add the lemon juice, glycerine and half the remaining sugar. Beat well until smooth and very white.
3. Gradually beat in enough of the remaining icing sugar to give a consistency which will just stand in soft peaks.
4. Put the icing into an airtight container or cover the bowl with a damp cloth and leave for several hours, if possible, to allow most of the air bubbles to come to the surface and burst.
5. The icing is now ready for coating a cake or it can be thickened, for piping stars, flowers, etc., with more sifted icing sugar or thinned down, for flooding, with lightly beaten egg white or strained lemon juice.

## ROYAL ICING – HOW TO FLAT ICE A CAKE READY FOR DECORATION

*Approximate quantities of icing sugar used to make royal icing for two thin coats on square and round cakes*

| SQUARE | | 15 cm/6 inch | 18 cm/7 inch | 20 cm/8 inch | 23 cm/9 inch | 25 cm/10 inch | 28 cm/11 inch | 30 cm/12 inch |
|---|---|---|---|---|---|---|---|---|
| ROUND | 15 cm/6 inch | 18 cm/7 inch | 20 cm/8 inch | 23 cm/9 inch | 25 cm/10 inch | 28 cm/11 inch | 30 cm/12 inch | |
| *Icing sugar* | 450 g/1 lb | 575 g/1¼ lb | 675 g/1½ lb | 900 g/2 lb | 1 kg/2¼ lb | 1.25 kg/2½ lb | 1.4 kg/3 lb | 1.6 kg/3½ lb |

Some people prefer to ice the top of the cake first and then the sides; others do it the other way round. It doesn't really matter so long as you add several thin coats rather than one thick coat, as this gives the smoothest surface. It is wise to apply the icing in sections rather than all in one go, allowing each application time to dry before continuing.

An ordinary royal iced cake requires two coats on the top and sides. Sometimes an extra coat on the top is necessary if it is not as smooth as you would like. A wedding cake, however, requires three coats all over, with an extra coat on the top for the lower tiers.

## TO ICE THE TOP OF THE CAKE

1. Place the cake on a cake board, attaching it with a dab of icing. Put a quantity of icing in the centre of the cake and smooth out with a palette knife, using a paddling movement. Remove surplus icing from the edges.

2. Draw an icing ruler or long palette knife across the cake towards you carefully and evenly, keeping the ruler or knife at an angle of about 30°. Take care not to press too heavily or unevenly.

3. Remove surplus icing by running the palette knife around the top edge of the cake, holding it at right angles to the cake.

4. If not sufficiently smooth, cover with a little more icing and draw the ruler or knife across the cake again until smooth. Leave to dry.

## TO ICE THE SIDES

Place the cake on an icing turntable if possible, or use an upturned plate.

**For a round cake**, spread a thin but covering layer of icing all round the sides of the cake. Again use a paddling action to push out as much air as possible, keeping the icing fairly smooth.

Hold an icing comb or scraper or a palette knife at an angle of about 45° to the cake. Starting at the back of the cake, with your free hand slowly rotate the cake, at the same time moving the comb slowly and evenly round the sides of the cake. Remove the comb at an angle and fairly quickly so the join is hardly noticeable.

Lift any excess icing from the top of the cake using a palette knife, again rotating the cake. If not sufficiently smooth, wipe the comb and repeat. Leave to dry.

**For a square cake** the best way of achieving good even corners is to ice two opposite sides first, and then when dry to ice the other two. Spread some icing on one side, then draw the comb or palette knife towards you, keeping the cake still to give an even side.

Cut off the icing down the corner in a straight line and also off the top and base of the cake.

Repeat with the opposite side and leave to dry. Repeat the process with the two remaining sides, keeping the corners neat and tidy, and leave to dry.

## SECOND AND THIRD COATS

1. Repeat the same method for the top and sides when applying each subsequent coat, but make sure each layer is dry before adding the next or you may disturb the previous coats. This will take about 3–4 hours, but can vary according to the room atmosphere.

2. Leave the cake to dry, uncovered, for 24 hours before adding the decoration.

## TO ICE THE CAKE BOARD

Complete the base icing of the cake and leave to dry. Stand the cake on an icing turntable and coat the board with a thin layer of icing (it may spread more easily if thinned slightly with a little egg white or lemon juice). Either run a palette knife round the edge while revolving the cake or hold an icing comb at an angle to the icing while rotating. Remove surplus icing from the edge of the board with a palette knife. With a square cake use the same method but ice two opposite sides, leave them to dry then complete the other two sides.

# BUTTER CREAM ICING

*Makes sufficient to coat the top and
sides of an 18 cm/7 inch sandwich
cake or fill and cover the top of the
cake*

*Preparation time: about 10 minutes*

100 g/4 oz butter or soft (tub)
margarine

175–225 g/6–8 oz icing sugar,
sifted

few drops of vanilla essence

1–2 tablespoons milk, top-of-the
milk, evaporated milk or lemon
juice

This standard recipe can be coloured and
flavoured in many ways to complement
the type of cake to be iced or filled.

1.  Cream the butter or margarine until soft.
2.  Beat in the sugar a little at a time,
adding the vanilla essence and sufficient
milk or lemon juice to give a fairly firm but
spreading consistency.

**VARIATIONS:**

*Coffee Butter Cream:* omit the vanilla
essence and replace 1 tablespoon of the
milk with coffee essence or strong black
coffee; or beat in 2–3 teaspoons instant
coffee powder with the icing sugar.

*Chocolate Butter Cream:* add 25–40 g/1–
1½ oz melted plain chocolate; or dissolve
1–2 tablespoons cocoa powder in a little
hot water to give a thin paste, cool and
beat into the icing.

*Orange or Lemon Butter Cream:* omit the
vanilla, replace the milk with orange or
lemon juice and add the finely grated rind
of 1 orange or lemon.

*Mocha Butter Cream:* dissolve 1–2
teaspoons cocoa powder in 1 tablespoon
coffee essence or strong black coffee and
add in place of the milk.

**Butter cream icing; Rich butter cream; Apricot glaze;
and at the top, Confectioner's custard**

*Brandy (or other liqueur) Butter Cream:* omit
the vanilla essence and replace the milk
with brandy, whisky, rum, sherry or any
other liqueur. A few drops of an
appropriate food colouring can be added.

*Almond Butter Cream:* replace the vanilla
essence with almond essence and beat in
about 2 tablespoons very finely chopped
toasted almonds.

*Walnut Butter Cream:* beat in 25–50 g/1–2 oz
very finely chopped walnuts.

*Apricot Butter Cream:* omit the vanilla
essence and milk and beat in 3 tablespoons
sieved apricot jam, a pinch of grated
lemon rind and a squeeze of lemon juice.

*Minted Butter Cream:* replace the vanilla
essence with peppermint essence. A few
drops of green food colouring and 3 or 4
crushed minted chocolate matchsticks can
be added, too.

# RICH BUTTER CREAM

*Makes sufficient to fill and cover the top of a 20 cm/8 inch sandwich cake*
*Preparation time: about 10 minutes*

75 g/3 oz butter
1 egg yolk
225 g/8 oz icing sugar, sifted
1 tablespoon flavouring (orange or lemon juice, coffee essence, etc.) or milk

1. Gently melt the butter in a saucepan. Remove from the heat and beat in the egg yolk.
2. Gradually beat in the icing sugar, alternating with the flavouring or milk until the mixture is light and fluffy.

# CONFECTIONER'S CUSTARD

*Makes about 450 ml/¾ pint*
*Preparation time: 10–15 minutes*

300 ml/½ pint milk
50 g/2 oz caster sugar
20 g/¾ oz plain flour
15 g/½ oz cornflour
1 egg
1 egg yolk
few drops of vanilla essence
knob of butter

1. Gently heat the milk in a saucepan.
2. Preferably using a whisk, beat the sugar, flour, cornflour, egg and egg yolk together until smooth and creamy. Beat in a little of the hot milk.
3. Beat the mixture into the rest of the milk in the saucepan and cook gently, stirring continuously, until the mixture thickens and just comes to the boil.
4. Stir in the vanilla essence and butter and cook gently for a few minutes longer, still stirring.
5. Remove from the heat and place a piece of cling film or wet greaseproof paper on the surface of the custard to prevent a skin forming. Leave to cool as quickly as possible. The custard can be stored in a refrigerator for up to 48 hours.

**VARIATION:**
*Almond Custard:* stir a few drops of almond essence into the sauce in place of the vanilla essence and add 40–50 g/1½–2 oz ground almonds.

# APRICOT GLAZE

*Preparation time: about 5 minutes*
*Cooking time: about 5 minutes*

175–225 g/6–8 oz apricot jam
2–3 tablespoons water

The cooled glaze can be stored in an airtight container in the refrigerator for up to 1 week, but it must be boiled and cooled again before applying it to a cake.

1. Put the jam and water into a saucepan and heat gently until the jam has melted, stirring occasionally.
2. Rub through a sieve and return to a clean pan.
3. Bring back to the boil and simmer until the required consistency is obtained. Allow to cool.

# EQUIPMENT & TECHNIQUES

Before you begin, assemble the basic items of equipment which you will require. Probably many of these will already be in your kitchen:

A selection of bowls and basins (of china or glass)
600 ml/1 pint measuring jug
set of measuring spoons
tablespoons and teaspoons
nylon sieves
wooden spoons
spatulas
pastry brush
kitchen scissors
large and small palette knife/spreader or a round bladed knife
icing ruler
icing comb or scraper (for sides of cakes)
skewers
string
rolling pin
small bowls with airtight seals
greaseproof, waxed, non-stick silicone papers and aluminium foil
selection of basic icing nozzles including fine, medium and thick writing, small, medium and large stars, rosette, ribbon and small petal

As your interest grows and you become more skilful, you may want to add the following to your icing equipment:

icing turntable
icing nails or a cork impaled on a skewer
metal or plastic templates
pair of compasses and/or cake markers
fine paint brushes

When buying equipment it is advisable to buy the best because it will last. Most equipment is widely available from large departmental stores, hardware shops, speciality kitchenware shops and from various cake decorating schools, or by writing to one of the mail order sources (addresses given at the back of this book).

A selection of **cake tins** is necessary and these should be made of a good firm metal. If you can, try to collect a set of tins that graduate in size at 2.5 cm/1 inch intervals (always measuring across the base of the tin). Tins that are round, square, hexagonal, horseshoe, heart-shaped, etc., are all available in graduating sizes, and other shapes including numerals are also readily available. If you require an unusual shape, try writing to one of the specialist mail order sources or icing schools who may be able to help; otherwise bake the cake in a large tin and cut it into the required shape using a paper pattern as a guide (see pages 35, 100 and 101 for details of shapes).

Some of the newer cake tins, particularly the larger deep ones used for rich cakes, measure a little larger than those which have been available for many years. This is due to metrication and whereas, for example, the old type of 7 inch tin measured nearer 6½–6¾ inches the new tins measure around 7¼ inches. This means that some recipes will produce a slightly shallower cake when baked in these new tins and they may need a slightly shorter cooking time.

It is a good idea to keep a few **wooden spoons** aside, especially for royal icing. Wooden spoons are better than metal but in general use they can become tainted with strong-smelling food and have stains which could be transmitted to the icing with horrific results!

A straight-edged **icing ruler**, preferably made of stainless steel, makes it much easier to smooth the top of a royal iced cake. The edge is completely smooth and once you get used to applying the correct amount of pressure to the ends of the ruler, smooth royal icing becomes simple.

Plastic **icing combs** or **scrapers** are used for the sides of cakes. They are smooth or serrated-edged and can be used equally well with royal icing or butter creams. They are simply pulled round the sides of a cake beginning at the back (with the cake preferably on a turntable) until smooth.

An icing **turntable** is essential when royal iced cakes are attempted regularly, although an upturned plate will suffice for the beginner. A heavy turntable is best, and one which remains stable when tilted for decorating the sides of cakes.

**Greaseproof, waxed and non-stick silicone papers and aluminium foil** are widely used. Always buy the best quality: you don't want it to split at a vital moment. Run-outs are done on non-stick silicone paper and chocolate work can be done on non-stick silicone or aluminium foil. Waxed paper is ideal for separating run-outs and models once dry.

**Greaseproof paper icing bags** are by far the simplest to use for all types of icings, and any size nozzle can be used with these paper bags. Greaseproof paper icing bags are ideal for piping small quantities of icing and it is a good idea to make several of these bags at a time. Do not overfill the bag; instead open it carefully and refill it when necessary, taking care not to split it or let it unfold. The filled bag can be kept in a polythene bag for a few hours, while completing another decoration.

# HOW TO MAKE A PAPER ICING BAG

1. Cut a piece of good quality greaseproof paper to a 25 cm/10 inch square. Fold in half to form a triangle.
2. Fold the triangle in half to make a smaller triangle (A to B) and press the folds firmly.
3. Open out the smaller triangle and fold the bottom half of the triangle (B) up to the folded line (C), creasing firmly.
4. Continue to fold the bag over (D to F) and then C to A, still creasing firmly.
5. Secure the join (A to E) with clear sticky tape or fold the top point (A) over twice to secure. Cut about 1 cm/½ inch off the tip of the bag and open out to insert the nozzle.

Apart from paper icing bags there are nylon bags and icing pumps.

**Nylon icing bags** are sold in varying sizes, from small up to extra large. They are ideal for large quantities of mixture and are easy to manipulate, but do not overfill or use a bag too large for the icing. Nylon bags can easily be refilled.

Apart from the large vegetable type of nozzle, which is fitted straight into the nylon bag, both plain and screw-on nozzles are available (see page 30). The plain type needs both a screw connector and a collar attachment. The screw connector is inserted in the bag, then the nozzle placed over the end and the collar attachment brought over the nozzle and screwed into the connector. With a screw-on nozzle the screw connector is inserted in the bag and the nozzle is screwed on the outside.

**Icing pumps** are usually bought as part of an icing set, complete with nozzles and often an icing ruler, turntable, etc. The pumps are sometimes made of metal, but are more often of polythene. They consist of a large tube with a screw for attaching the nozzles at one end and a plunger with holes for two fingers at the other end. This is easily unscrewed for refilling the tube and dismantling for washing. An icing pump is cumbersome for very fine work. Its main disadvantage is that you can't 'feel' how the icing is reacting to the pressure of the plunger, so the icing may come out in fits and starts.

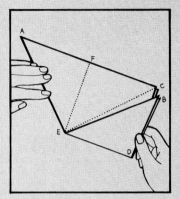

Folding bottom of triangle (B) to (C)

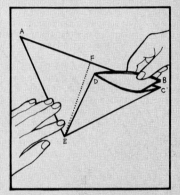

Continuing to fold bag (D) to (F)

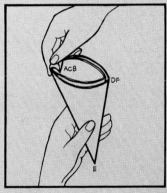

Securing join

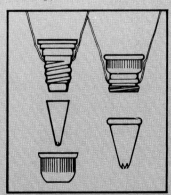

Bottom: Nylon icing bags with a plain nozzle (left) and a screw-on nozzle (right)

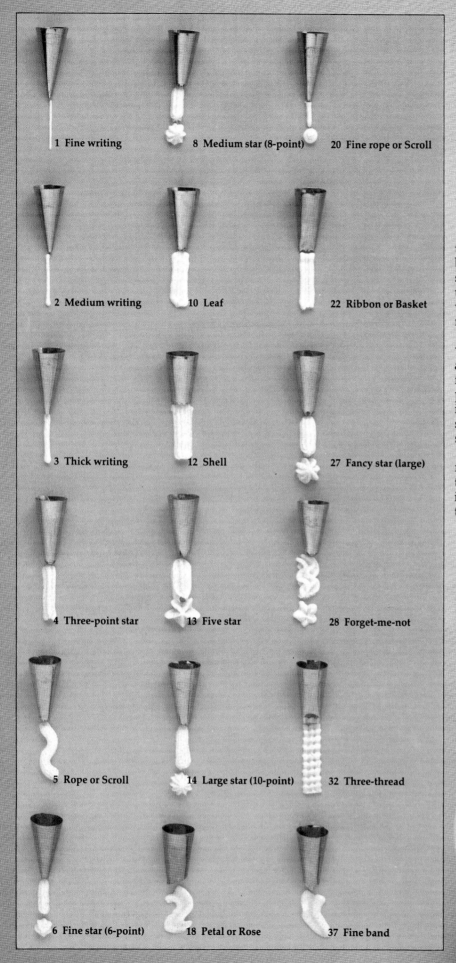

1 Fine writing

8 Medium star (8-point)

20 Fine rope or Scroll

2 Medium writing

10 Leaf

22 Ribbon or Basket

3 Thick writing

12 Shell

27 Fancy star (large)

4 Three-point star

13 Five star

28 Forget-me-not

5 Rope or Scroll

14 Large star (10-point)

32 Three-thread

6 Fine star (6-point)

18 Petal or Rose

37 Fine band

**Piping nozzles** are also known as tubes and pipes. There is a large range available, in both plain and screw-on types, covering all styles. They are sold by number which can be confusing because not all the manufacturers use the same number for the same shaped nozzle. So always check on that particular manufacturer's chart before buying. Screw-on nozzles are specially for use with icing pumps or nylon piping bags. Although screw collar nozzles can also be used in paper icing bags plain nozzles are best because they fit neatly into the bag.

Make sure when you select nozzles that they are perfectly shaped, with no dents or badly fitting seams. For example, mis-shapen points of rosettes will give unevenly piped stars and writing nozzles which are slightly oval instead of perfectly round will affect the resulting design.

Larger nozzles, often called 'large', 'vegetable' or 'meringue' nozzles, are available in metal or plastic. They are used for piping whipped cream, mashed potato, meringues, éclairs, etc. They come in a range of sizes, plain, rope and star-shaped, and are often used on gâteaux or something needing a heavy decoration.

Although, as already stated, not all the manufacturers of nozzles conform with their numbering system, the numbers illustrated are the same with at least two of the makes and similar to others.

# PIPING TECHNIQUES

With all icing, practice makes perfect. Once piped, royal icing becomes hard and is unable to be used again, so if you are a complete beginner try practising with a nylon piping bag filled with reconstituted instant mashed potato, using the varying shapes of vegetable nozzles. The potato can be scooped up many times and re-used until you get the 'feel' of handling a piping bag. Even when you are using royal icing, if you are not quite sure or are trying out a new design, practise an edging, border or writing on something other than the cake. An upturned cake tin is ideal and the icing will soak off easily in warm water.

Decorations other than those actually piped on to the cake should be made at least 24 hours in advance. Base iced cakes are also best left uncovered at room temperature for 24 hours before beginning the decorations.

## PREPARING THE ICING BAGS

If using a paper icing bag (see page 29), cut about 1 cm/½ inch off the tip and insert the nozzle. Half to two-thirds fill the bag with icing, using a small palette knife or teaspoon to push it well down into the bag, then fold over the top carefully, continuing to push the icing down to the tip. Do the same with a nylon bag after fitting the special screw collar connector and nozzle, but do not put in too much icing or the bag will be difficult to manipulate. The easiest way to fill a nylon bag is to place the nozzle between the finger and thumb of your left hand and fold the rest of the bag over your hand so it is inside out; in this way as you spoon in the icing with the right hand it can be pressed down to the tip by the left hand and the outside of the bag stays free of icing.

## HOLDING THE ICING BAGS

You will soon know how you prefer to hold the icing bag to make it work best for you, but here is the easiest way. For paper icing bags, open your hand and place the bag across your palm with tip towards the ends of your fingers. Place the thumb on the folded end of the bag (to keep in the icing), then fold over the other four fingers to hold the bag tightly. Use the other hand to steady it and apply a steady pressure to the bag until the icing begins to come out of the nozzle. With a nylon bag, place the thumb and forefinger round the icing in the bag and twist the bag tightly two or three times to prevent the icing coming out or moving up the bag. Then hold the bag

tightly over the twist, again with the thumb and forefinger, with the rest of the fingers folded over the bag. Apply pressure with the other hand.

Alternatively, for fine work and lattice hold the bag in both hands with the thumbs over the end, and the rest of both hands supporting the weight underneath.

## CONSISTENCY OF ICINGS

It is most important to use icing of the correct consistency for the job in hand. Royal icing varies with the type of icing to be done. For dots, shells, rosettes, etc., it should be stiff enough to stand in well formed but not hard peaks, but for writing or trellis it must be slacker or the icing will constantly break. However, it must not be too soft or it will not hold its shape. Glacé icing for piping lines, lacework, writing, etc., needs to be stiffer than that used to coat a cake: simply add extra sifted icing sugar. Butter cream should be stiff enough to pull into softish peaks, but not too firm or it will not pipe evenly. Butter cream can be used to work designs of shells, stars, rosettes, etc., on a cake.

## FOOD COLOURINGS

Liquid colourings, in many concentrated colours, are readily available. However, because the many different makes of blue colouring vary in shade it is advisable carefully to compare the bottles when buying this colour, to avoid disappointment. Shades can vary from turquoise to a purple tone and it is difficult to find a true blue.

The easiest way to add any colouring, a little at a time, is to dip a skewer into the bottle of colouring and add a few drops to the icing.

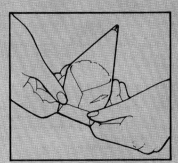
**Folding the end of a paper icing bag**

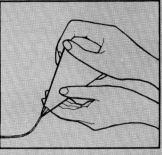
**Holding a paper icing bag**

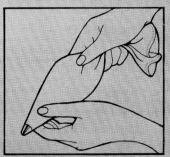
**Holding a nylon icing bag**

**An alternative way of holding a nylon bag for finework**

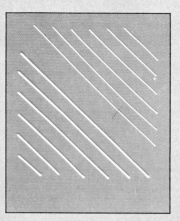

Fine and medium straight lines

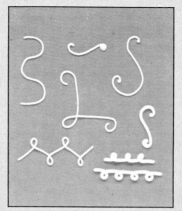

Curved lines

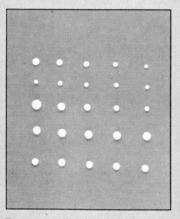

Thick straight lines

Writing

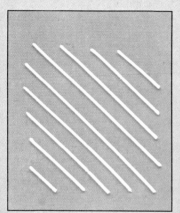

Dots

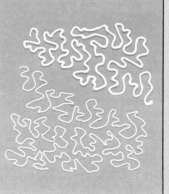

Lacework

Lattice

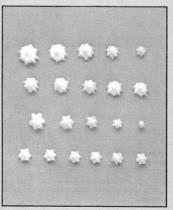

Stars

# USING THE NOZZLES

## PLAIN NOZZLES

Place the nozzle in the piping bag (fine, medium or thick writing) and fill with icing. Before you begin make sure the tip of the nozzle is wiped clean or it will not be easy to start the piping.

**Straight lines:** place the tip of the nozzle where the line is to begin. Press the icing out slowly and as it emerges lift the nozzle about 2.5 cm/1 inch above the surface. Move your hand in the direction of the line to be piped using the other hand to guide the bag and keeping the icing flowing evenly. About 1 cm/½ inch from where the line should finish, stop squeezing and bring the tip of the nozzle gently back to the surface. Break off the icing. By holding the icing above the surface it helps even shaky hands keep straight lines – with a little practice! Some people prefer to pipe lines towards them while others like to work from left to right or vice versa – it doesn't matter which you do. If you finish with a blob of icing at the end of a line, remove it carefully with a fine skewer or a small sharp knife.

**Dots:** hold the nozzle upright and just touching the surface. Squeeze the bag gently, at the same time lifting the nozzle to allow the icing to flow out. Stop squeezing when you have the size of dot you want and remove the nozzle quickly with a slightly shaking action, to avoid leaving a tail. Use a hat pin if a tail does remain. Dots can be made in all sizes and with any of the writing nozzles. Lines of two sizes of dots are attractive, as are graduating sizes down the side of a cake. Dots are used for overpiping on plain lines for added decoration, perhaps using a different colour. Two-tier dots can be formed by dipping the nozzle downwards into the icing halfway through, giving the dot a large base and small top.

**Lattice:** this is the most attractive way of using straight lines and can be worked in many ways. It is done by first piping a series of parallel straight lines in one direction, keeping them evenly spaced over the area of the cake to be covered. Leave to dry, then turn the cake and pipe a second layer of parallel lines over the first but at right angles or an angle of 45° to the first ones; this creates squares or diamonds. The design can be left at this but is better with a third layer piped over the first lines to give a raised and almost 3-D effect. With very fine lattice up to five layers can be worked. It is wise to let each layer dry before starting the next for then if a mistake is made, the wet layer can be easily lifted off with the help of a skewer or small sharp knife. Many other attractive lattice designs can be worked using curved lines, etc.

**Curved lines:** these can be worked quite easily, once you have mastered control of the icing, to produce curved decorations, loops, plain scrolls, etc. For curves you really need a template (see pages 36 and 37), and it is a good idea to practise on thin card or greaseproof paper. Draw a series of curves and pipe over these until you feel confident. Place the tip of the nozzle at the beginning of the curve, lift it up above the surface as for straight lines and allow the icing to follow the curve round, lowering the nozzle to touch the surface between each scallop. Also practise scrolls and other curved shapes you may need to use.

**Writing:** the design should be pricked or traced on to the cake to make sure it is central and will fit in. First write the words on greaseproof paper, then position on the cake and carefully prick out on the surface using a pin. When the paper is removed the guide lines for the writing remain. It is wise to pipe the words in white icing first and then, when dry, to overpipe with a colour – mistakes in colour on a white cake are difficult to cover up. Again practice is necessary and it is best to begin with capitals. All styles of writing can be used as you progress.

**Lacework:** using a fine or medium writing nozzle, this is a very effective decoration. It is like scribbling and can be added to set designs on cakes. Lacework is as easy to apply to the top of a cake as it is to the sides. Hold the nozzle almost upright and just above the surface so that the icing flows out and move the nozzle around quickly and easily to form the pattern.

## STAR NOZZLES

These vary widely in size and shape of the star they produce. Some have five points, others six or eight and even more points as they become larger. For beginners, concentrate on 5-point (no 13) or 8-point (no 8). Many designs can be made using star nozzles.

**Stars:** place a star nozzle in the bag and fill with icing of the correct consistency. Hold the bag upright and just above the surface. Pipe out sufficient icing to form the star and sharply lift the nozzle away with a down and up movement. Stars should sit fairly flat on the surface, not be pulled up into a point in the centre.

**Rosettes or whirls:** these are piped with the same star nozzles but in a circular movement like making a large dot. Begin just above the surface and move the nozzle in a complete circle to enclose the middle

and finish off quickly to leave a slightly raised point in the centre but not a 'tail'. These can be made in varying sizes and slightly differing shapes depending on which nozzle you choose.

**Shells:** use either a star nozzle or a special shell nozzle (no 12); both make good shells and are worked in the same way but the shell nozzle gives a rather fuller and fatter shell. Hold the icing bag at an angle to the surface and a little above it. Start in the centre of the shell and first move the nozzle away from you, keeping an even pressure of icing, then back towards you with a little more pressure for the 'fat' part of the shell. Release pressure and pull off sharply to form a point. To make a shell edging simply repeat the shells, linking them in a line by beginning the next shell over the tail of the previous one. It is very important to finish off each shell and lift the nozzle between each one or a bulky and uneven border will result.

**Scrolls:** these are useful for tops and sides of cakes but do need a lot of practice, particularly if you want to achieve graduated scrolls. A simple scroll edging can be worked using either a star or shell nozzle, but if they are to be larger or individual scrolls on the top of a cake, a template will ensure evenness (see pages 36 and 37). Hold the icing bag as for a straight line and with the nozzle almost on the surface. Work a question mark shape beginning with a fairly thick head and gradually releasing the pressure while finishing off in a long pointed tail. A series of scrolls can be worked the same way or several variations can be worked to make attractive designs or double-ended scrolls. Other scrolls can be worked adding twists and graduating the width and size, and using larger and smaller nozzles.

**Coils:** this is a border or edging and is made using a star nozzle. Begin just touching the surface and continue making small circular movements in an anti-clockwise direction. Coils can be worked from left to right or vice versa as you prefer, and variations of a coiled border are numerous.

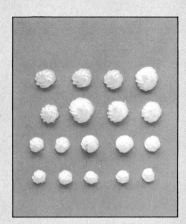

Rosettes or Whirls

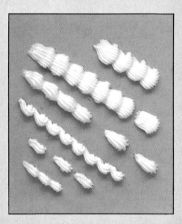

Shells

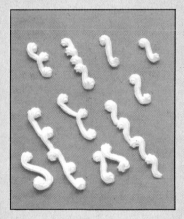

Scrolls

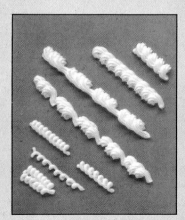

Coils

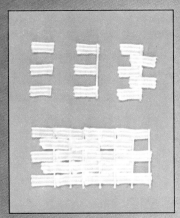

**Basket weaving**

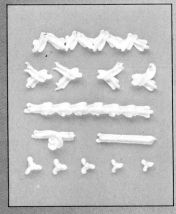

**Trefoil patterns**

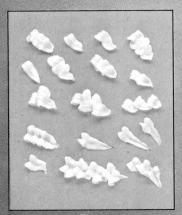

**Leaves**

**Building up the petals for a rose**

## RIBBON OR BASKET NOZZLE

This nozzle (no 22) is thick, with either one or both sides serrated and is flat to produce a ridged ribbon of icing. Some nozzles are evenly ribbed while others are of an uneven design. A ribbon nozzle is used for a flat pleated ribbon edging, which is worked continuously by simply overlapping each pleat, as well as for basket work or 'weaving' on a cake. To do the latter you require one icing bag fitted with a ribbon nozzle and another fitted with a medium or thick writing nozzle. Hold the ribbon nozzle sideways to the cake and at an angle and pipe three short lines the same length as each other, one above each other and with the width of the tip of the nozzle between each one. Pipe a straight vertical line with the writing nozzle along the edge of the three ribbon lines. Next pipe three more straight lines with the ribbon nozzle of the same length as the first ones to fill in the gaps but beginning halfway along those and covering the straight line. Pipe another vertical line at the end of these lines and continue building up first with the ribbon nozzle and then the vertical line until you join up with the start. Weaving takes practice but is quite easy once you get under way.

## THREE-POINT STAR NOZZLE (TREFOIL)

This nozzle (no 4) is used for borders or small stars on edges or at the base of cakes. It is unusual and very simple and can be worked either upright or upside-down. Make the stars in the same way as for an ordinary star nozzle.

## LEAF NOZZLE

This nozzle (no 10) has a pointed tip sometimes with an indentation in the centre of the point. You can also make your own leaves using just a paper icing bag with the tip cut off to give a point (see page 46). You can make three overlapping movements for each leaf or if this sounds a bit difficult, simpler leaves can be made in the same way but without the overlapping movement, and other shaped leaves can easily be devised. Leaves can be piped straight on to cakes, or on to non-stick silicone paper first. Leave to dry before attaching to the cake with a dab of icing.

## PETAL OR ROSE NOZZLE

This nozzle (no 18) is used specially for making flowers. Flowers are made separately, by piping each on to a small square of non-stick silicone paper attached with a dab of icing, to an icing nail, or a cork impaled on a skewer. The flower is left undisturbed until dry, when it can be removed and attached to the cake. The pieces of paper can be used repeatedly. Flowers need practice but you will gradually find they become easier to make. (To pipe a rose see page 44.)

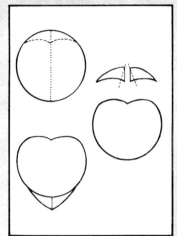

1. Making a heart-shaped cake

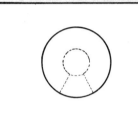

2. Cutting out a horseshoe shape

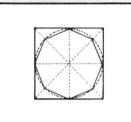

3. Making an octagonal cake

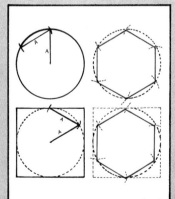

4. Making hexagonal cakes from a round and a square

# CUTTING DIFFERENT SHAPED CAKES

For a **heart-shape** bake a round cake and cut a paper pattern (diagram 1); the 'V' should be about 4 cm/1½ inches deep on a 20 cm/8 inch cake and gradually deeper on larger cakes. The piece taken out should then be cut in half and reversed to make the point at the base; a triangular piece will need to be trimmed off both sides to make it fit. Attach to the cake with Apricot Glaze (page 27).

To make a **horseshoe** cake, bake the size required in a round cake tin. Using a paper pattern first cut out a central circle of cake about 5 cm/2 inches on a 15–18 cm/6–7 inch cake, 7.5 cm/3 inches on a 23–25 cm/ 9–10 inch cake and gradually enlarge the central hole as the size of the cake increases. Then cut a wedge-shaped piece from the top (diagram 2).

For an **octagonal** cake (eight-sided) bake a square or round cake a little larger than required, then cut off each corner evenly to give the eight sides (diagram 3). A **hexagonal** cake (six-sided) is a little more complicated and wasteful but can be made from a round or square cake with the help of a pair of compasses (diagram 4). Other shapes can be devised with a little thought and the surplus cake cut off makes a treat for teatime in advance of the party.

# TEMPLATES

When you begin to design a cake think about the top decoration. If it is going to include shaped lines you will need a pattern, or template. These can only be used on a hard icing such as Royal Icing (page 24) or Gelatine or Moulding Icing (pages 20 and 21). Metal or plastic symmetrical rings and cake markers are available, but you can also make your own templates very simply to create your own designs.

Templates are first drawn on greaseproof or other paper with the help of compasses, set square, ruler, etc. Start with a square or circle about 2.5 cm/1 inch smaller in width than the cake, depending on the size of the cake. The template must be exact and symmetrical in all ways because if it is only a little off-shape the whole design of the cake will be spoiled. Once you have prepared the design it can be transferred to thin card and cut out ready to use time and again. Cut a 'V' in the centre to make it easy to lift off from the top of the cake.

Place the prepared template on top of the flat iced cake. Mark the outline of the design by pricking around or through the card or paper with a pin (if using stiff card prick around it). A template can also be used on the sides of a cake, especially if the design includes curves or scallops which must be kept even. Don't forget that with tiered cakes you need to make similar graduated templates to fit each size.

Using a fine or medium writing nozzle (no 1 or 2) pipe round the template as closely as possible over the pinpricks. With straight lines break the icing at corners to give sharp points and keep curves and joins of scallops even. When complete and dry, carefully lift off the template by the 'V' in the centre. Pipe a second line of icing on top, either in white or a coloured icing.

Other designs and decorations can be added freehand; it is only the basic design that requires the template. The area left between outlines can be left plain or be decorated with lacework, lattice, flowers, scrolls, etc.

## TO MAKE A BASIC TEMPLATE FOR A ROUND CAKE
1. Cut a circle of greaseproof paper.
2. **For an eight-point decoration** fold the circle in half, then into quarters and again into eighths, creasing the folds firmly.
3. **For a six-point decoration** fold the circle first in half and then carefully into three, making sure each piece is exactly even (a pair of compasses make this easier).

## TO MAKE A BASIC TEMPLATE FOR A SQUARE CAKE
1. Cut a square of greaseproof paper.
2. **For a four-point decoration** fold the square in half diagonally to give a triangle, then in half again to give a smaller triangle.
3. **For an eight-point template** fold in half a third time to give a still smaller triangle.

**Making a Hilary template using a square of paper**

## DESIGNS SUITABLE FOR ROUND AND SQUARE CAKES

For round and square templates draw the chosen design on the top piece of the folded circle or square using a pencil, then cut the line exactly with a pair of scissors. Open out to check the design is even and correct before use or transferring to card.

**Star:** Use a circle of paper and mark a point about 2.5 cm/1 inch down the open side of the paper (longer for larger cakes) and draw a straight line to the top edge of the folded side.

**Scallop:** fold a circle or square of paper into eight points and draw a scallop.

**Pointed petal:** fold a square of paper into quarters and then into eight points. Keep the fold to the left and make a mark 5– 10 cm/2–4 inches (depending on size of cake) down the right-hand side. Draw a deep curved arc to the point of the fold.

**Hilary:** (as used on page 64). Use a circle or square of paper and fold to eight points. Keep the folded edge to the left and draw a shallow curve to come about half way across the paper; then draw a second shallow curve to go almost straight to the open edge.

**Curved:** both concave and convex curves are suitable. Use a circle of paper, fold into eight points and draw a curve across the end.

**Heart:** use a circle of paper and fold into eight points. Fold in half again to find the centre of the heart and mark a point 2– 4 cm/¾–1½ inches down the fold. Draw the heart shape from this point round to the other edge.

**Eliza** (as used on page 64): use a square of paper and fold into quarters. Keep the folded edges downwards and cut out a semi-circle from the top corner.

**Turret:** fold a square into eight points. Beginning at the outer open edge draw two downward steps towards the opposite edge. The sizes of the steps can be varied for different designs, or make just one step.

**Petal:** use a circle of paper and fold into eight points, then fold again and mark the centre of each section at the edge. Draw and cut out a deep petal shape coming to the mark.

**Laura** (as used on page 67): use a circle or square of paper and fold into eighths. Cut out a scroll or scallop, beginning about 2.5 cm/1 inch down the fold and ending about 2.5 cm/1 inch along from the corner on the curved edge.

**Fleur** (as used on page 66): use a circle of paper and fold into six points. Cut out a concave curve. For a **Hexagon** cut a straight edge across the top.

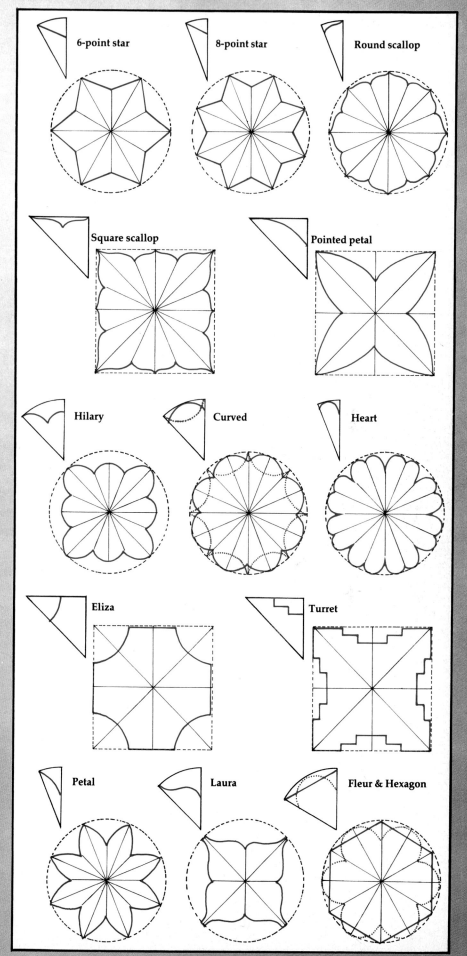

# SIMPLE DECORATIONS

This section gives ideas for simple and speedy ways of filling, icing and decorating everyday cakes, sponge sandwiches, slab cakes and quick and easy birthday cakes.

## FILLING THE CAKE

Place the cake layer on a wire rack or plate. Spread the filling – jam, butter cream, frosting, whipped cream, etc. – evenly over the cake using a round-bladed knife or palette knife. Take the filling right out to the edge of the cake; be generous with the filling but not over-generous. Position the second cake layer on top and press down until even, then brush off any loose crumbs.

## DECORATING THE SIDES OF THE CAKE

If the sides are to be iced or decorated it is best to do this before touching the top as it prevents disturbing the decorations once complete. The sides on many cakes are best left plain, but for a more professional finish they may be coated with chopped or flaked nuts, coconut, grated chocolate, etc.

Brush or spread the sides with a little Apricot Glaze (page 27), or spread with a thin layer of Butter Cream (page 26 or 27) if the top is to be covered with butter cream. Put the chosen coating on a sheet of greaseproof paper. Holding the cake carefully on its side, roll in the coating until well covered. About 75 g/3 oz chopped nuts or grated chocolate will be required to coat the sides of an 18–20/7–8 inch sandwich cake.

For a patterned side simply spread a thicker layer of butter cream around the sides and use a serrated icing comb or scraper, fork or palette knife to make a pattern.

## DECORATING THE TOP OF THE CAKE

### SUGAR TOPPING
Select a paper or plastic doily with a fairly large pattern and put it on top of the cake. Dredge the cake heavily with sifted icing sugar or caster sugar, then very carefully lift off the doily to reveal an attractive pattern.

### BUTTER CREAM TOPPINGS
These can be spread or piped straight on to the top of a cake although a layer of apricot glaze will help with a cake which has a particularly crumbly surface. Both apricot glaze and a thin layer of marzipan can be added first, if preferred. The following are some suggestions for butter cream toppings:

1. For a simple topping, cover the top of the cake as evenly as possible with butter cream using a round-bladed knife. Make sure you don't pull any crumbs up into the icing. Draw the knife slowly backwards and forwards across the butter cream, slightly overlapping the previous line each time to give even spaces between each line, until complete. Arrange nuts, sweets or chocolate shapes, etc., around the edge of the cake to complete.

2. Spread an even layer of butter cream over the top of the cake, then with the round-bladed knife make swirling lines from the centre of the cake to the edge all the way round. Piped rosettes of butter cream and a nut or glacé cherry will complete the decoration.

3. Spread a smooth layer of butter cream on top of the cake and mark into diamonds or squares with a sharp knife, wiping clean after each cut. Alternatively, pipe lines to give these shapes using a butter cream in a contrasting colour or darker shade and a fairly thick plain writing nozzle. A small decoration can be added to some of the squares.

4. A serrated icing comb or scraper can be pulled round the butter cream on the top of the cake, either evenly or with indentations to give a scalloped effect. A piped shell edging, made with a medium star nozzle, or piped rosettes and chocolate shapes can finish off an elegant yet simply made topping.

5. 'Rough up' the butter cream with a fork, back of a spoon or small palette knife. This surface can be sprinkled with nuts, grated chocolate or coconut, etc., or be decorated in any other way you like.

## GLACÉ ICINGS

Speed is of the essence here, so all the decorations required must be ready before you begin: once the cake is iced it sets very quickly and will crack if disturbed. Ice the top of the cake, leaving the sides plain or coated (see left), or ice the whole cake.

For the top, make the Glacé Icing (page 20) and when it is thick enough to coat the back of a wooden spoon and very smooth, pour it over the middle of the cake. Using a round-bladed knife spread it out quickly and evenly over the top almost to the edge. If the icing drips over the edge, quickly remove it with a knife or leave until set and then cut off. Alternatively, tie a piece of non-stick silicone paper all round the sides of the cake to come about 2.5 cm/1 inch above the top of the cake. Pour on the icing, spreading to the edge where the paper will hold it to shape while it sets. Remove the paper very carefully when set.

To coat the whole cake in glacé icing, place it on a wire rack over a plate and pour almost all the icing over the middle of it. Spread the icing out evenly, allowing it to run down the sides. Use a palette knife dipped in hot water to help the icing cover the sides; fill in any gaps with the icing left in the bowl. Leave to set, then trim off drips from under the rack and remove the cake carefully. Add decorations (except butter cream piping, see below) before the cake begins to set and do not move until completely set.

If decorating with butter cream, the glacé icing must be allowed to set hard first. The top can be decorated with piped butter cream rosettes, shell edgings, etc., and a border can be piped around the base of the cake if it is iced all over. A trellis or lines can also be piped using a medium writing nozzle and butter cream that is a little thinner than usual.

Lines, dots or lace work can also be worked in glacé icing, provided it is made stiffer than usual, or use cooled melted chocolate. Use a paper icing bag (page 29) and cut off the tip to the required size.

**Feather icing** is a most attractive finish for sandwich cakes, pastries and biscuits. It must be done very quickly before the first layer of glacé icing begins to set or the effect will not be so dramatic.

Ice or coat the sides of the cake first, if this is to be done. Next make the amount of glacé icing required for the top of the cake and leave it white. Make up a second quantity of icing using 50 g/2 oz icing sugar and colour it fairly brightly. If the top is to be white the feathering must be a good contrasting colour. Alternatively, if the top is to be dark or coloured then the feathering can be white.

Put the smaller quantity of glacé icing into a greaseproof paper icing bag. Use the other icing to coat the top of the cake (see left). Cut the tip off the icing bag and pipe straight lines across the top of the cake at 1–2 cm/½–¾ inch intervals. Immediately draw a skewer or the point of a knife across the lines at right angles about 2–2.5 cm/¾–1 inch apart. Quickly turn the cake round and draw the skewer across again in between the first lines but in the opposite direction to complete the feathered effect. Leave to set.

Another feathered design is made by piping the contrasting colour in a continuous spiral on top of the cake, beginning in the centre and working outwards to the edge. Draw the skewer from the centre of the cake to the edge, marking it into four quarters, then draw the skewer from the outer edge to the centre between the first lines to complete the pattern.

## OTHER ICINGS

Frostings and other icings (see the Icings, Frostings and Fillings section) can be used to decorate cakes very simply but effectively. All types of decorations can be added before the frosting or icing has set. Again it is wise to have these ready before you begin as frostings in particular set very quickly.

Some simple cake decorations:
Left: Decorating the sides with chocolate; Sugar topping; Right: Butter cream topping; Feather icing

# MAKING SIMPLE DECORATIONS

Use these with butter cream and glacé icing or frostings.

## NUTS

Use walnut halves, pecan halves, hazelnuts (toasted or plain), almonds (blanched, split, flaked, etc., and plain or toasted) or pistachio nuts (blanched to give the best green decoration).

## COCONUT

Use it desiccated, shredded or in long strands. Leave it plain, toast it, or tint it any colour you like to represent sand, sea, grass, etc. To tint coconut, soak it in warm water with a few drops of liquid food colouring added until the required colour is achieved. Drain well and dry on paper towel before using.

## SUGAR-FROSTED FLOWERS AND FRUIT

Use small spring flowers, heathers, roses, etc., as well as herb leaves, and fruits such as small apples, pears, grapes, cherries, redcurrants, segments of mandarin oranges, etc. Put 1 egg white in a small bowl with 2 teaspoons cold water and whisk until lightly frothy. Make sure the flower heads or fruit are clean and dry, then paint all over with or dip into the egg white until evenly coated. Sprinkle with or roll in caster sugar, then leave to dry on greaseproof paper lightly dusted with sugar. When dry, store between layers of tissue paper for 3–4 weeks.

## CRYSTALLIZED FLOWERS

These are very attractive and keep well if made with care. Real flowers can be used as decorations at any time of year, instead of making them from marzipan or a moulding icing. Use fairly small flowers, such as primroses and violets, which are not quite fully open and remove all bruised petals and leaves. With bulkier flowers, such as roses, the petals can be crystallized individually and rearranged into flowers again. Herb leaves such as mint crystallize well too.

There are two methods of crystallization. For the first, put 120 ml/4 fl oz triple strength rose water into a screw-topped jar with 50 g/2 oz gum arabic crystals (both available from certain chemists) and leave overnight or longer, giving an occasional shake until the gum arabic crystals have dissolved. Hold the flower carefully by the stem (the stem can be removed when the flower is crystallized) and using a fine paint brush, paint the rose water mixture all over the petals on both sides. Quickly dredge or roll in caster sugar, making sure the flower is completely covered, then shake off surplus sugar. Place on a wire rack or on greaseproof or non-stick silicone paper and leave to dry in a fairly warm place for 1–2 days. Pack carefully between layers of tissue paper to store.

For the second method, melt 450 g/1 lb loaf or granulated sugar in a large heavy-based saucepan. Bring to the boil, then strain through scalded muslin into a clean pan to remove any impurities. Bring back to the boil and boil to 104°C/220°F on a sugar thermometer. Leave to cool to about blood heat. Arrange the flowers on a wire rack over a shallow tin and pour the sugar syrup over each flower, using a fine paint brush to ensure all the flower is coated. Drain off excess syrup, then leave the flowers undisturbed in a warm place for 12–18 hours or until crystals begin to form on the surface. This means that crystallization is taking place. Pack away carefully as above.

## CHOCOLATE DECORATIONS

Many effective decorations can be made with chocolate. There are many types of chocolate which can be used for chocolate work and decorations but the plain varieties are always easier to handle because they set firmer than milk chocolate and have a harder texture. Special cake covering chocolates and unsweetened blocks of bitter chocolate are also suitable and easy to use. The latter are obtainable from some cake specialists. Plain couverture chocolate has an excellent flavour but is much more expensive. Packets of chocolate dots are popular as an alternative and are easy to handle. Remember though that a drop of water or other liquid in chocolate whilst it is melting, in particular the cake covering chocolates, will change the texture.

The simplest way to use chocolate is to grate it on a fine, medium or coarse grater for the top and/or sides of cakes and small cakes. Almost as simple is to make **'mock' chocolate curls** by peeling thin strips off a block of chocolate using a potato peeler. Chill the curls after making, and use to decorate the sides of cakes or gâteaux. These curls are quicker to make than the true chocolate curls below.

**Chocolate curls** are made by spreading a thin layer of melted chocolate on a firm surface, such as Formica or marble. Leave until just firm but not set hard. Using a straight-bladed sharp knife hold the knife at the point and at the handle and place

Chocolate curls

Chocolate leaves

Chocolate cut-outs

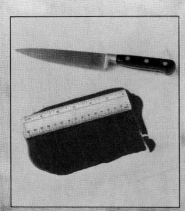
Chocolate squares and triangles

across the chocolate at an angle of about 45°. Gently draw the knife towards you, carefully shaving off a curl of chocolate. Take care not to cut too deeply into the chocolate or it will not curl. Place the curls on a plate and chill. Store in a container between layers of waxed paper.

**Chocolate leaves:** chocolate cake covering is the best to use; ordinary plain or milk chocolate is not so easy to manage. Break the chocolate and put it into a heatproof basin. Place over a saucepan of gently simmering water, not fast boiling, and heat gently until melted. Take care not to get any water into the chocolate or this will ruin the texture. Remove from the heat and stir until smooth. Select good shaped, perfect rose leaves (or other attractive leaves). Wash and dry them carefully. Using a fine paint brush, coat the underside of the leaves with melted chocolate. Place the leaves, chocolate side upwards, on a plate and chill until set, then carefully peel off the leaves. Store in a small container in the refrigerator for up to 2 weeks.

**Chocolate cut-outs:** melt about 50 g/2 oz chocolate cake covering (as above) and spread out thinly on a piece of silver foil or non-stick silicone paper. Pick up the corners of the foil or paper and drop gently on to a flat surface to level the chocolate. Leave the chocolate until barely set. To make petals, moons and curved triangles use a 4 cm/1½ inch and a 2.5 cm/1 inch plain cutter to cut out chocolate rounds. (Larger or smaller cutters may be used.) Cut the larger rounds into four triangles with a sharp knife. Using the smaller cutter, cut each remaining round in half to form a moon and petal shape. Place on a plate and chill. Store in a small container in the refrigerator for up to 2 weeks. To keep the shapes shiny, handle them as little as possible.

**Chocolate squares and triangles:** draw a 15 cm/6 inch square on silver foil or non-stick silicone paper. Melt 50 g/2 oz chocolate cake covering (as above) and spread thinly within the marked square.

**Right: Piped chocolate shapes and making chocolate Easter eggs**

Pick up the corners of the foil or paper and drop gently on to a flat surface to level the chocolate. Leave until just set. Using a ruler and sharp knife, trim the chocolate to the marked square, then cut into nine 5 cm/2 inch squares (or larger or smaller squares). Cut the squares in half to make triangles. Place on a baking sheet and chill until hard. Store in a small container in the refrigerator for up to 2 weeks.

**Chocolate Easter eggs:** these are fun to make and the small ones make good decorations for the tops of Easter cakes. Moulds are available in plastic, metal and china, and in various sizes. They can be obtained through the makers of a chocolate cake covering as well as from kitchen hardware stores and specialist kitchen equipment and gadget shops. Brush the inside of the mould with melted chocolate to give it an even layer, then chill until set. Repeat with another coat on small eggs or two further coats on larger ones. Chill thoroughly, then remove the eggs from the moulds.

**Piped chocolate shapes:** spread melted chocolate on silver foil or non-stick silicone paper as for chocolate squares and cut into ovals, rectangles, elongated triangles, etc. when set. Chill until hard. Put a contrasting melted chocolate (plain on milk chocolate shapes or vice versa) into a greaseproof paper icing bag (see page 29), cut off just the very tip and pipe squiggles on the shapes. Leave any extra chocolate in the bag, then when hard peel off the paper and store ready for future use.

### GLACE CHERRIES
Use whole, halved, cut into quarters or sliced.

### SWEETS
Use jellied orange and lemon slices cut to the size required, chocolate drops, chocolate beans. Cake decorations, such as mimosa balls and sweet flowers, are also available ready-made.

### ANGELICA
These candied stems of the angelica plant can be cut into all manner of shapes and sizes and make excellent 'leaves' to put with 'flowers' for decorations.

# SIMPLE DESIGNS FOR BIRTHDAY CAKES

### CARTWHEEL CAKE
Cover the top with butter cream or glacé icing, keeping it smooth. Using a contrasting colour and a thick writing or medium star nozzle, pipe 'spokes' from the centre of the cake almost to the edge. Then pipe a thick edging to the cake for the outside of the wheel. Decorations can be put between the spokes.

### CLOCK CAKE
Cover the top with butter cream or glacé icing. Using a medium writing nozzle pipe the numbers of the clock face evenly round the top of the cake. A chocolate button can be added to make the numbers stand out more. Then pipe the 'hands' of the clock, possibly pointing to the appropriate number for the age of the child. An edging of icing can also be added and extra decorations as required.

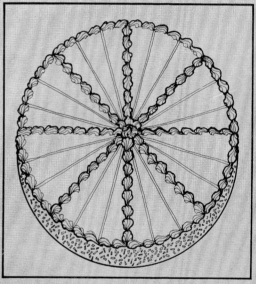

Cartwheel

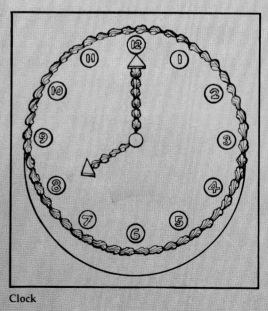

Clock

### LITTLE COTTAGE

Cut the top two corners from a square cake, then cover it all over with butter cream or glacé icing. Use chocolate buttons to 'tile' the roof; windows and a door can be marked by piping on a contrasting butter cream. Bought or homemade flowers or sweets can be added for a border of flowers for the garden. Shutters are best made from licorice sweets. A piped number or a decoration on the door can represent the age of the child.

### CHECKERBOARD

Mark the cake top lightly into squares with a knife. Make two contrasting colours of butter cream and put each into a piping bag fitted with a medium star nozzle. Fill alternate squares with one colour either by piping a continuous line backwards and forwards or with stars of icing touching. Fill the remaining squares with the second colour. An edging can be added to the cake, and chocolate peppermint creams can be used to represent counters.

### DAISY CAKE

Spread a thin layer of butter cream on the cake or cover with glacé icing and leave to set. Using white or a pale colour of butter cream outline seven or eight 'petals' on the cake. Fill these in with stars or shells or continuous piped lines. Use a contrasting colour or a group of small sweets for the centre of the flower.

Little cottage

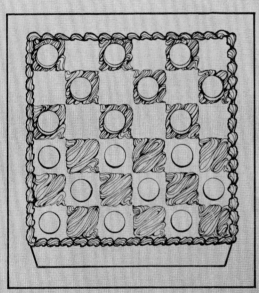

Checkerboard

Daisy

# SPECIAL DECORATIONS

Distinct from the simple decorations described in the previous section are those made separately and attached to the cake when dry. These decorations include piped flowers, all types of models, cut-outs and run-outs. They are made from Royal Icing (page 24), Gelatine Icing or Moulding Icing (pages 20 and 21) and Marzipan (page 22). All these decorations can be made 3–4 weeks in advance. They should be covered with tissue or waxed paper and kept in a dry atmosphere once they are completely dry.

Royal icing is used for piped flowers and leaves of all types, and for run-outs. In most of the modelling, moulding or gelatine icing and marzipan are interchangeable.

It is easier to colour moulding icings to obtain true or bright colours because you start with a white base; but marzipan will turn a good colour too, particularly if you use a white or natural coloured variety. This is available from some shops or by post from icing specialists, or it can be made at home (see page 22). Knead food colourings into icing or marzipan until the mixture is evenly coloured and no longer streaky. If the icing or marzipan becomes too soft or sticky, extra icing sugar may be added. For dark colours use the concentrated colourings, which are available from specialist icing centres. A touch of brown colouring or gravy browning will tone down an over bright colour. Extra colour or features can be painted on by using a fine paint brush and liquid food colourings.

For rolling out, use a surface lightly dredged with icing sugar or a mixture of icing sugar and cornflour, or roll out between sheets of polythene or waxed paper. The latter method makes it easier to move the rolled-out icing or marzipan.

Egg boxes are a great help for resting models and flowers on as you make them. Wooden cocktail sticks, and a fork are other useful implements.

The flowers, models, cut-outs and run-outs here are featured on cakes throughout the book. Some other designs, not given in this section, will appear under particular recipes.

## PIPED FLOWERS IN ROYAL ICING

All icing takes practice, but making flowers takes a lot of practice – and patience – until you feel confident and can make all sorts of different flowers with ease. Roses are probably the most popular flower to make and are a good start if you are a beginner. There are numerous other flowers which you can make by following instructions or by making your own shape.

To make flowers you need an icing nail or a cork impaled on a skewer, a quantity of non-stick silicone or waxed paper cut into 2.5–5 cm/1–2 inch squares, and a paper or plastic icing bag fitted with a large, medium or fine petal nozzle. For most flowers use a medium nozzle, which is the easiest to obtain and the easiest to use. Half fill the bag with icing and fold down ready to begin. Secure a square of paper to the icing nail with a dab of icing.

### ROSE
Hold the piping bag so the thin edge of the petal nozzle is upwards. Squeezing evenly and twisting the nail at the same time, pipe a tight coil for the centre of the rose. Continue to add five or six petals, one at a time, piping the icing and twisting at the same time, but taking each petal only about three-quarters of the way round the flower. Begin in a different part of the flower each time to keep the shape even and keep the base of the nozzle in towards the centre of the flower or the rose will expand at the base and the top and lose its shape. The petals can be kept tight to form a rosebud or opened more for full-blown flowers. One or two really open petals can be worked at the bottom of the flower. The larger flowers can have more petals and should be worked with the largest petal nozzle. Often a tiered wedding cake will have the sizes of roses graduated, with tiny ones on the top tier working down to large roses on the bottom. Leave all roses to dry for about 24 hours before removing from the paper and when dry store in an airtight container until required.

## NARCISSUS

This is a flat flower so begin with the thick edge of the petal nozzle to the centre. Keep the nozzle flat, and work each petal separately. Gently squeeze out the icing, take the tip outwards to a point, still keeping it flat, then bring it back towards the centre, twisting it slightly and gradually releasing the pressure; break off. This gives one petal. Make five more in the same way, each slightly underlapping its neighbour, by placing the nozzle just under the previous petal as you begin to pipe. Leave to dry, then add the centre using yellow or orange icing and a small petal nozzle. Pipe a cup right in the centre of the flower by making a complete circle of icing while rotating the nail. Leave to dry, then using a fine paint brush dipped in orange colouring just tint the edges of the cup. Pipe dots of yellow in the centre of the cup for the stamens.

## PRIMROSE

You need pale yellow icing for this pretty flower. It is a five-petalled flat flower made in a similar way to the narcissus, but the petals are almost heart-shaped. When the nozzle is out from the centre, instead of bringing it straight back, dip it towards the centre and then take it out again before returning completely to the centre. This will give the required heart shape. Complete the flower with four more petals and leave to dry. Work a few tiny dots in the centre using a fine writing nozzle and deep yellow or pale orange icing.

## CHRISTMAS ROSE

This rose is another flat flower made in a similar way to the narcissus but the petals are tilted slightly upwards at the edges and rounded to the 'tea-rose' shape. The centre is filled with a lot of pale to deeper yellow dots for the stamen. For **lenten lilies** the stamen can be yellow or pale mauve and the centre of the petals can be tinted pale mauve using a fine paint brush and mauve and pink liquid food colourings.

## DAISY

Probably the simplest of the piped icing flowers, the daisy is also the most effective. Pipe five or six or more slightly rounded but also pointed petals, each separate from its neighbour. Then using a medium writing nozzle pipe a large dot in the centre of the flower (if preferred several dots can be piped) using a contrasting colour. These flowers can be made in a variety of colours either with the petals one colour and the centre white or yellow, or the petals white with a coloured or yellow centre.

## PANSY

Another five-petalled flower, this is a little more complicated with the petals worked in a different order. It is not always easy to obtain the correct coloured icing for these flowers and it helps to copy the colourings of real flowers. Using a medium petal nozzle pipe two flat rounded petals, underlapping the second. Then work the next two petals slightly on top of the first two and a little larger. Turn the flower around 180° and work another larger petal to complete the flower. Leave to dry. Pansies can be worked in yellow, mauve, deep red, etc., and some flowers can be a mixture with the first two petals in, say, yellow and the remainder mauve. When dry paint deeper shades of mauve food colouring in the centre of the flower and complete with a few dots of yellow icing for stamen.

## VIOLET

The most difficult part of this flower is to get a really deep mauve icing – try mixing deep pink, mauve and possibly a touch of brown. Work the same way as a pansy, but making the first four petals smaller and more pointed. Finally turn the flower round 180° and pipe a larger elongated petal. Add fine dots of green icing to the centre for stamen.

## SIMPLE FLOWERS

Small sprays of flowers and tiny individual flowers can be piped straight on to a cake, after first practising on a plate. Try lily of the valley, forget-me-nots and ornamental flowers of no particular variety with small leaves. A writing nozzle – fine or medium – and a fine star or 5 star nozzle are best for these flowers.

## LEAVES

There is a special piping nozzle available for piping leaves. They can be made separately or be piped straight on to the cake. Leaves can be worked in white or in varying shades of green, but for wedding cakes they are most often white. However, on other formal cakes a touch of green often improves their appearance.

It is easier to use the special leaf piping nozzle, but you can also manage without one by using a greaseproof paper icing bag (see page 29) and cutting the tip off in a special way. First fill the bag as usual. Then press the end flat between the thumb and finger and cut the point off in an inverted letter 'V' like the head of an arrow.

Begin with the nozzle or paper bag touching the cake (or square of paper) and the end turning up a fraction. Press gently and as the icing begins to come out of the bag, raise it slightly. When the leaf is large enough, break the icing off quickly leaving a point. The bag can be gently twisted or moved up and down to give different shapes and twists to the leaves and the size can be increased by extra pressure. Leave to dry. A variation is to make three overlapping movements for each leaf, pulling the point away sharply after the last one to leave a point.

For a leaf edging to a cake, work each leaf separately on the cake, working backwards round the edge so the leaf tips overlap and are left showing. If some

**Above: Greaseproof paper icing bags cut ready for piping leaves**

larger leaves are required simply cut a larger 'V' shape. To obtain a vein effect on the leaves, use small pointed scissors to make a tiny cut into the centre of the 'V'. A surprising number of different leaves can be made with a little practice.

# MOULDED DECORATIONS

To assemble the various shapes use egg white with marzipan models, or use a dab of the icing with gelatine or moulding models.

### ELEPHANT

Large elephants require about 75 g/3 oz of pink moulding or gelatine icing or marzipan. Shape two-thirds of it into a cylinder and bend to form into front legs, body and back legs. Split the legs to form two rounded feet back and front. Roll a piece into a ball and then pull out a trunk at one end. Shape two large ears from flat circles and a tail from the trimmings. Attach the head, ears and tail to the body. Complete features with white royal or glacé icing to give tusks and toes, and pink or silver balls for eyes.

### LION

Use 25–75 g/1–3 oz yellow marzipan or moulding icing. Use just over half to shape into a cylindrical body with legs apart. Divide each end to make front and back legs. Use a small piece for a tail with a thick knob at one end, and attach to the body. Roll most of the remainder into a ball for a head and attach; half a cocktail stick through the head and body will secure it. Finally, roll minute pieces into rolls with pointed ends about 2.5 cm/1 inch long and attach for the mane. Leave to dry slightly, then using a fine paint brush and brown liquid food colouring paint on a face, stripes down some of the mane, feet and dark hairs at the tip of the tail.

### CAT AND FIDDLE

Use 40 g/1½ oz marzipan to make a cat (see page 48), with a small piece shaped into a fiddle bow.

### TIGER

Similar to a lion, this beast is made from 25–75 g/1–3 oz orange marzipan or moulding icing. Use three-quarters for the body and shape the remainder into a tail and cat-like head with pointed ears. When partly dry, paint on stripes all over the body and back of the head with brown or black food colouring or gravy browning. Then paint on the face.

### RABBIT

Use 40 g/1½ oz brown marzipan or moulding icing. Shape two-thirds into the body of an upstanding rabbit, then shape the remainder into two long ears, four feet, and a head with a pointed nose. Stick the head on to the body followed by the ears and feet. Use a dot of white marzipan or icing for a tail and add white tips to the feet. Mark eyes with icing.

### LEOPARD

Use 50 g/2 oz white marzipan or cream-coloured moulding icing. Shape three-quarters of it into a cylinder with long legs. Slit the front and back piece to shape into legs and feet. Use a small piece to shape into a tail; attach to the body. Use the remainder for the head which should be cat-like with sharp pointed ears and a fairly thick neck; attach to the body. When partly dry, paint on dots of a dark bluish-brown or black colour using liquid food colourings; also paint a nose and eyes.

### MOUSE

This can be made from any amount of brown (or other coloured) marzipan or moulding icing, from 15 g/½ oz up to 75 g/3 oz. Remove a small piece to roll into a tail, then shape the remainder into a body with a small piece one end to make the head and ears and a thicker rounded piece for the back. Mark on the back legs and tiny front feet. Attach the tail and add silver balls or specks of chocolate for eyes.

## CAT

Use 50 g/2 oz orange, black, brown or natural coloured marzipan or moulding icing. Mould two-thirds into a long cylinder. Fold one-third under the rest of the body for the back legs and split the other end in half to form paws. Shape a ball for the head from most of the remaining marzipan with two pieces pinched up for ears. Attach the head to the body and fold one front paw over the other. Roll the rest of the marzipan into a tail and attach to the body, curling it up over the cat's back. Paint toes on the paws and features on the face with a fine paint brush and brown liquid food colouring or gravy browning.

## DOG

Use 40–50 g/1½–2 oz marzipan or moulding icing made any suitable colour. Use three-quarters of it to make a cylinder and shape into a body with fairly short legs with feet. Use a tiny piece to shape into a pointed tail. Use the remainder to make a head and two rounded ears to stick on to the head. Assemble the body, head and tail and leave to dry slightly. Paint on eyes and a nose with brown liquid food colouring or gravy browning.

## WINNIE THE POOH CHARACTERS

Each character requires about 25 g/1 oz white or natural coloured marzipan, of which almost 15 g/½ oz is shaped into a 4 cm/1½ inch circle for each animal to stand on. Once attached, the circle should be painted with green food colouring to represent grass.

**Eeyore:** colour the remaining marzipan a deep mauve/grey and mould into a donkey shape with a drooping head and thick tail. Add chocolate vermicelli for his mane and the tip of his tail and a minute piece of any coloured marzipan for 'the nail' which keeps his tail on! Mark eyes with a flake of chocolate and finally add two small flopping ears of the same marzipan down each side of his head. Attach to the circle of marzipan and leave to dry.

**Tigger:** colour the remaining marzipan orange and shape into a lying down tiger, giving him two out-stretched paws in the front, a head with pointed ears and a long curling tail. The back legs and feet can be marked and shaped out of the body. Paint stripes all over with brown liquid food colouring or gravy browning. Attach to the circle of marzipan and leave to dry.

**Winnie the Pooh:** colour the remaining marzipan yellow and shape a bear with a round head, two pinched-up rounded ears, two arms and two legs in a sitting position. A tiny pot of honey can be placed in front of him on the circle of marzipan. Paint on his nose, eyes and an 'H' on the honey pot with brown liquid food colouring, and his paws and the honey pot lid with red colouring.

**Christopher Robin:** use 25 g/1 oz white or natural marzipan for the boy and about 15 g/½ oz for the oval of 'grass' for him to lie on. First shape two legs, one bending upwards from the knee, then two arms, one to rest his head on with a bend at the elbow, and a head. Colour about 15 g/½ oz marzipan blue or turquoise and use to shape a body. Another small piece can be coloured red or orange to make an open book. Put the 'body' on the oval of marzipan, position the legs and arms and then stick on the head. Chocolate vermicelli can be stuck on for hair. Paint the soles of the feet and shoes with brown liquid food colouring and mark features on the face. Position the book in front.

**Kanga:** colour the remaining marzipan a brownish/red colour and mould into an upright kangaroo with a fairly pointed head, four paws and a flat tail. Use white or cream icing to give her a white tummy and a dot for each eye. Attach to the circle of marzipan and leave to dry.

## REINDEER

Use about 50 g/2 oz brown marzipan. Shape one-third for a body; use another third to shape four legs about 4 cm/1½ inches long. The remainder is for a tiny tail, a head with a thick neck and two pairs of antlers. Assemble carefully. Add white icing eyes and spread or pipe icing down the neck from under the head right under the tummy to the tail. Leave to dry.

## FATHER CHRISTMAS

About 50 g/2 oz marzipan is required. Colour a small ball pink for the face. Colour a little more brown and use to make two flat 'boots' and a sack to put over his shoulder. Tint the rest of the marzipan a bright red. Remove a small piece and shape into a hat and two smaller pieces still for arms. The remainder should be made into a body with a fat tummy and two bulky trouser legs. Attach the boots to the base of the legs, arms to the body and head with the hat on top. Use white royal icing to pipe 'fur' round the base of the trousers, down the front of the jacket, round the waist, around the cuffs and on the hat. Complete with facial features and a large beard. Finally throw the sack over his shoulder, attaching with a dab of icing. Leave to dry.

## SLEDGE

Use about 40 g/1½ oz yellow marzipan. Remove a small portion and colour it green. Shape the yellow piece into a sledge shape with a flat base and sides which stand up about 4 cm/1½ inches at the back down to about 1 cm/½ inch at the front. Crumpled waxed paper can be put inside the sledge to hold it in shape while it dries. Roll out the green marzipan and cut out pieces to decorate the outside of the sledge. Attach them with water.

## MARY, MARY, QUITE CONTRARY

Use about 50 g/2 oz white or natural coloured marzipan. Remove a knob and roll into a head. Remove another small piece and roll out thinly to use for the apron. Tint a minute piece brown and roll into two plaits and a little hair and attach to the head. Tint the rest of the marzipan a bright red. Use two tiny pieces for bows on the plaits. Roll two pieces into arms and roll out another thin piece for a hat. Roll the remainder into a cylinder with a fuller base to represent the skirt. Stick the head on, and attach the plaits and hat. Cut a pinafore out of the white marzipan and wrap it round the model. Finally, attach the arms and paint features on the face. Leave to dry. A watering can may be formed out of a green or brown piece of marzipan and a selection of flowers for the garden made from scraps of coloured marzipan. Leave to dry and store very carefully.

## BOY

Use about 50 g/2 oz white or natural coloured marzipan for a sitting or standing model. Roll a small ball for a head. Colour a small piece brown, roll out a little piece thinly, add to the head for hair and rough up with a fork. Roll the rest of the brown marzipan to make two shoes. Tint just under half the remainder one colour and shape into an upper body with two arms. Colour the remainder blue or turquoise and use to form the lower body with one leg bent at the knee in a sitting position and the other bent to rest over the first leg as for the Gone Fishing Cake on page 87. Sit the boy on the edge of a book or an egg box to help keep his sitting position. Attach the rest of the body, including shoes. Leave to dry, then paint on facial features. Make a standing boy in the same way except for the legs.

## GIRL

Similar to Mary, Mary, but omit the hat and apron. The lower part of the body – the skirt – can be a different colour from the top part of the body and the legs should be natural coloured the same as the face. Shoes can be brown or to match the skirt. A small basket made in brown marzipan can also be made to go with her.

## MOULDED FLOWERS

**Rose:** these can be made from marzipan, moulding icing or gelatine icing and are probably one of the most popular cake decorations. Choose a rose colour or shades of this colour – or make white roses if using the moulding or gelatine icing.

For the basic shape of the rose first make a solid cone of mixture about 1 cm/½ inch overall. Roll out the remaining mixture very thinly and cut out a circle about 1 cm/½ inch in diameter. Hold the circle at one side and with the other hand carefully press out the rest of the circle until very thin and almost transparent. Carefully wrap round the cone with the thick part at the base, attaching with a dab of water or egg white, if necessary. Continue to make three or four more petals, attaching carefully and curving slightly to give a realistic rose shape.

For a small rose four petals are sufficient, but for larger ones add a few more petals cutting the circles a little larger as necessary. Take care not to press the central core too firmly or into a point, or the flower will become too elongated and look more like a cabbage than a rose. Dry carefully on non-stick silicone or waxed paper and store each rose separately on a piece of waxed or tissue paper. Do not attach brightly coloured flowers to white royal iced cakes until both are quite dry, or the colour may seep on to the white icing. It may take several days for these flowers to dry thoroughly.

**Rose leaves:** roll icing out thinly and cut into leaf shapes.

**Narcissus or daffodil:** use differing shades of yellow or white marzipan for these; some of the central trumpet can be made from orange marzipan. The basic shape requires five or six petals and a central trumpet with a stamen in the centre. Use a circle for the trumpet and twist it so the lower part protrudes more than the top of the trumpet; then put a tiny cone-shaped piece in the centre for the stamen. Attach the petals round the outside of the trumpet, bending them to give a realistic shape. Leave to dry, then paint round the mouth of the trumpet with orange liquid food colouring and a fine paint brush.

**Violet:** colour some marzipan a deep mauve and a small amount yellow. This flower has four or five petals and each one is shaped from a small circle. Press the edges of the circle so it doesn't have a cut edge. Mould the first circle into an open cone shape. Add three similar sized petals round the top of the flower, pressing the bases together. The last petal should be a little larger than the others and is placed under the centre and away from the other three petals. Make four tiny stamens from yellow marzipan and stick into the centre of the flower.

**Fuchsia:** here the colours can range from white through shades of pink and mauve to a deep ruby red. Each flower is made from two colours, e.g., pink and deep pink, mauve and red, white and pink, two shades of mauve, etc, and each has a long stamen of yellow or green. With the first colour, cut out four petals in a normal petal shape with a rounded top. Gently mould the edge of the top of each so it is not a sharp cut; wind these round the long stamen making sure there is an elongated base as the whole flower tends to be long. Then with the contrasting colour cut out four sharp pointed petals. Arrange these round the centre of the flower, attaching one at a time to give an open flower; the petals should all bend slightly backwards.

**Primrose:** cut out small fluted circles of thinly rolled-out pale yellow marzipan. Using a small sharp knife, make five small cuts almost into the centre to form the petals. The edges of the petals can be pressed out slightly to give a thinner edge. Press the centre firmly to close the flower up slightly. Make small balls of pale orange marzipan and arrange about five in the centre of each flower. Leave to dry. Leaves can be made from a pale green marzipan to give long oval shapes with a slightly frilly edge made by cutting unevenly, once shaped; mark with veins.

**Daisy:** make six to eight narrow pointed petals of any coloured marzipan and arrange in a circle so they all touch. Pinch the centre together gently. A centre of yellow or a contrasting colour is made by adding first a tiny circle of marzipan and then lots of minute dots stuck on to this centre piece.

**Simple flowers:** non-descriptive flowers can be made very simply by cutting out circles of coloured marzipan and moulding them round a small ball of yellow marzipan. The edge of each circle can be cut into petals or simply pinched into points or curves. Another way is to cut a fluted circle, pinch it a little in the centre (or leave it flat) and put a single ball of contrasting coloured marzipan in the centre. This type of flower can be altered and devised in many ways.

# MARZIPAN FRUITS

**Banana:** roll a little yellow marzipan into banana shape with one end blunt and the other end tapering off. Paint on brown stripes and markings using liquid food colouring or gravy browning.

**Apple:** roll natural coloured or pale green marzipan into small balls and make slight indentations at the top and base. Cut off the tip of a clove and use for the calyx at one end and the stem at the other. Alternatively, use coloured marzipan. If using green marzipan, paint part of the apple with red food colouring blending it gradually into the green. With natural coloured marzipan first paint with red and then blend in with green colouring.

**Pear:** use a little natural coloured marzipan and form into a pear shape with a pointed tip and fat rounded base. Add a stem and calyx as for apples, and then paint the pear with green and brown liquid food colouring to give the desired effect.

**Cherries:** use red or natural coloured marzipan and shape into balls with a slight indentation at the top. Add a piece of angelica for the stem. With natural coloured cherries paint part of the fruit with red colouring.

**Orange and lemon:** use orange and yellow marzipan for these, shaping oranges round and lemons slightly elongated. To achieve the texture of the skin either prick all over with a pin head or roll on a grater. Add cloves or coloured marzipan for the calyx.

**Strawberries:** mould deep pink/red marzipan to the correct shape of a strawberry with a pointed tip and rounded top with a slight indentation. Roll in granulated sugar to represent the seeds and make a hull from green marzipan.

**Plum:** use deep yellowish-red or deep plum coloured marzipan and shape into an oval plum. Make a cut down one side of the fruit and add a clove for the stem.

**Grapes:** make tiny balls of pale green or mauve marzipan and stick together to form a bunch of grapes. Add a clove for the stem.

# CUT-OUTS

### CHRISTMAS TREES

Draw a pattern for a simple Christmas tree to the required size. Cut out in rolled-out green marzipan. Cut out a small piece of rolled-out red marzipan for a tub and attach to the tree. Leave to dry on waxed or non-stick silicone paper. For a more decorative tree cut out a second tree somewhat smaller than the first and stick it on top of the first one. When dry, the tip of the tree branches can be decorated with dots of icing and/or silver or coloured balls to represent baubles.

### HOLLY LEAVES AND BERRIES

Make a dark green-coloured marzipan by adding a touch of brown colouring for the leaves, and a small piece of deep red marzipan for the berries. Roll out the green marzipan thinly to a strip and cut into rectangles about 2.5–4 cm/1–1½ inches long and 2 cm/¾ inch wide. Using a tiny round cutter or the base of a piping nozzle take cuts out of the edges of the leaves. Mark a vein down the centre with a knife, and leave to dry, putting some leaves over a wooden spoon handle to give a curved shape. For the berries roll tiny pieces of red marzipan into balls and leave to dry.

### IVY LEAVES

Draw several sizes of ivy leaves on paper and cut out, or use real ivy leaves for the pattern if you can find them. Place on thinly rolled-out marzipan (not quite such a dark green as for holly) and cut out the leaves. Mark veins with a knife and leave to dry, again putting some over a wooden spoon handle or rolling pin to give curved leaves.

### MISTLETOE

This is made from an even paler green marzipan and the leaves are cut into long thin tongue shapes with rounded ends. Mark a heavy vein down the centre with a knife and leave to dry. White mistletoe berries can be rolled from white or natural coloured marzipan.

### VARIOUS LEAVES

A great variety of marzipan leaves can be made. Rose leaves are popular and for other varieties either look around the garden or stop and look into a florist's window. Many different shapes and sizes can be made and the marzipan tinted in varying shades of green.

### HORSESHOES

Instead of using bought horseshoes you can create your own in marzipan, moulding or gelatine icing, or royal icing. Decide on the size you want, then draw a pattern on paper and cut out. Use marzipan or icing coloured as you want and roll it out, keeping it a little thicker than for leaves. Mark 'nails' with the prong of a fork and leave to dry.

### STARS

Draw patterns of stars in the sizes you require and cut out of rolled-out yellow marzipan. Either five- or six-pointed stars can be used. When dry they can be decorated with dots of icing at the points or fine lines of icing to outline or simply mark the corners; white or yellow icing looks good.

# RUN-OUTS

Run-outs, made from royal icing, can be piped straight on to a cake or on to non-stick silicone paper or waxed paper and attached to the cake when dry. They make attractive raised designs to lay flat or stand upright on a royal iced cake. The chosen shape is first outlined by piping and then filled in with softer icing. They are suitable for freehand drawings, tracings, writing, emblems, numerals, etc, or for plaques which can have a further decoration piped or placed on top.

Run-outs are very fragile and it is wise to make several 'extras' in case of breakages. They are difficult to repair and there may not be sufficient time left to make a new run-out at the last minute.

All run-outs can be made in any colour icing. Simply add liquid food colouring from the tip of a skewer. Remember only a tiny bit of food colouring will be needed when tinting a small amount of icing. When the run-outs are completely dry attach to the cake with more royal icing.

First draw the outline on a piece of card. Lay non-stick silicone or waxed paper over the drawing, attaching firmly with pins or a dab of icing. Using a fine writing nozzle (no 1, or no 2 for a large run-out) trace round the outline of the drawing. Leave to dry. Thin down a little royal icing with lightly beaten egg white or strained lemon juice until it just flows. Spoon into the centre of the outline and let the icing flow out to fill the outline completely, using a skewer to help guide it. For small outlines or awkward shapes, put the flowing icing into a greaseproof paper bag without a nozzle, cut off the end and pipe into the outline until filled. Prick any air bubbles which appear with a pin. Leave to dry for 2–3 days. A further outline or features can be piped on top of the run-out using a writing nozzle, or star or shell nozzle.

For butterflies, draw small butterfly wings on non-stick silicone or waxed paper, like the shape of a 'B' and about 2 cm/¾ inch long. Outline and fill in the shapes, as described. On non-stick silicone or waxed paper pipe a 'body' with a medium writing nozzle, the same length as the wings. Leave to dry. Attach the wings to the body with icing and allow to dry. Complete with a second coat for the body, between the wings.

For a plaque on a cake, prick out the shape to be covered, then outline it and when dry flood with flowing icing. Leave to dry thoroughly. This makes an attractive centrepiece on a tiered wedding cake. Make sure to mark the position of the pillars before making the plaque: the icing used for the plaque may not take the weight of another cake and might crack.

# CELEBRATION CAKES

Royal Icing (page 24) and, to a lesser extent, Gelatine and Moulding Icing (pages 20 and 21) are used to create smoothly iced celebration cakes, with simple or elaborate decorations. (For piping techniques see pages 31–34.) These special cakes are prepared for many occasions and often make the centrepiece for a party table.

A variety of cake shapes can be used – round, square, heart-shaped, horseshoe, hexagonal, etc. Tins are available for most shapes from specialist cake decorating suppliers, if local shops cannot oblige. However, it is expensive to buy a new tin for a shape that may be used only once or twice and it is possible to make your own special shape of cake from a basic round or square cake (see page 35).

With wedding cakes it is most important to make an even-sided cake of the correct proportions or the finished result may look top heavy or unevenly balanced. It must also be large enough to feed the expected number of guests. As a rough guide 450 g/ 1 lb baked cake, without marzipan or icing, should cut into about 10 portions when completed; therefore, for each 45–50 guests you will need around 2.25 kg/5 lb cake. If the top tier is to be saved, then remember to calculate the weight required from the lower tiers only. Square cakes weigh heavier than round ones of the same size and the cakes can be made deeper or shallower as required.

For two-tier cakes, either round or square, use one of the following (the number of portions includes the top tier):

| Tiers | Portions |
|---|---|
| 30 and 20 or 18 cm/ 12 and 8 or 7 inch | up to 160–200 |
| 28 and 18 cm/ 11 and 7 inch | up to 125–140 |
| 25 and 18 or 15 cm/ 10 and 7 or 6 inch | up to 100 |
| 23 and 15 cm/ 9 and 6 inch | up to 75 |

For three-tier cakes use one of the following combinations (here the top tier is NOT included in number of portions):

| Tiers | Portions |
|---|---|
| 30, 23 and 15 cm/ 12, 9 and 6 inch | up to 250 |
| 28, 20 and 13 cm/ 11, 8 and 5 inch | up to 150 |
| 25, 20 and 15 cm/ 10, 8 and 6 inch | up to 120 |
| 23, 18 and 13 cm/ 9, 7 and 5 inch | up to 90 |

Wedding cakes look best displayed on a silver cake stand. Instead of hiring or borrowing one, you can make a very adequate stand yourself with four thick cake boards about 5–7.5 cm/2–3 inches larger than the bottom cake board, stuck together with clear sticky tape. Tie a wide silver braid or silver and white ribbon round the sides to cover the joins.

Pillars are used to hold the tiers and they should suit the overall design. Choose round pillars for round cakes and square ones for square cakes. With two tiers use four pillars. Sometimes on three-tier cakes with a very small top tier three pillars will be sufficient on the middle tier.

The wedding cakes in this chapter are for one-, two- and three-tiered designs. When making more than one tier do not add glycerine to the royal icing for the first two coats of the bottom tier and the first coat of a middle tier (see page 24).

# HEART-SHAPED BIRTHDAY CAKE

*Preparation time: icing and decorating the cake*

1 × 20–23 cm/8–9 inch round Rich Fruit Cake (page 11), cut to a heart shape (see page 35)

1 recipe quantity Apricot Glaze (page 27)

675 g/1½ lb Marzipan (page 22)

Royal Icing, made with 1.4 kg/3 lb icing sugar (page 24)

peach food colouring

silver balls

3 Marzipan Fuchsia (page 50)

5 green Marzipan Leaves (page 52)

Instead of using the flowers and leaves as decoration a peach and/or silver ribbon bow can be placed on the top of the cake.

1. Brush the top and sides of the cake with apricot glaze, then cover with marzipan (see page 22). Leave to dry. Attach the cake to a silver cake board about 5 cm/2 inches larger than the cake with a dab of icing.
2. Tint the icing pale peach with food colouring. Use enough of this to flat ice the cake, giving it two coats all over and a third coat to the top if necessary (see pages 24 and 25). Leave to dry for 24 hours.
3. Prick out 'HAPPY BIRTHDAY' and the name on the top of the cake. Using a medium writing nozzle, outline and leave to dry.
4. Use the pale peach icing and a piping bag fitted with a medium writing nozzle to overpipe the writing.
5. With a deeper coloured icing and a fine star nozzle, pipe an individual shell edging all round the top edge of the cake and another border all round the base of the cake.
6. Pipe a straight line of stars all round the centre sides of the cake. Leave to dry.
7. With the paler icing and the writing nozzle, pipe a looped design from shell to shell round the bottom edge of the cake. Position a silver ball at the point of each iced loop.
8. Pipe another looped design from star to star (or every alternate one) all round the side of the cake, again adding silver balls.
9. Position the marzipan flowers and leaves above the writing on the top of the cake and attach with icing.

# SPORTING BIRTHDAY CAKE

*Preparation time: icing and decorating the cake*

1 × 20 cm/8 inch square Rich Fruit Cake (page 11)

1 recipe quantity Apricot Glaze (page 27)

800 g/1¾ lb Marzipan (page 22)

Royal Icing, made with 1.25 kg/ 2½ lb icing sugar (page 24)

yellow food colouring

little egg white, lightly beaten, or lemon juice, strained

1. Brush the top and sides of the cake with apricot glaze, then cover with marzipan (see page 22). Leave to dry. Attach the cake to a 25 cm/10 inch square silver cake board with a dab of icing.

2. Tint two-thirds of the icing yellow with food colouring. Use to flat ice the cake, giving it two coats all over and a third coat to the top if necessary (see pages 24 and 25).

3. Draw the outline of two crossed cricket bats and two crossed tennis rackets, a yacht or other type of boat, or a car about 5 cm/2 inches high on a sheet of paper. These sporting motifs can be drawn freehand, or by tracing a picture of the correct size. Place the drawings under a sheet of non-stick silicone paper.

4. Using a medium writing nozzle and white icing outline the drawings five times each for bats and rackets or 9 times for boats or cars, moving the pattern under the paper each time.

5. Thin about 6 tablespoons of the icing with a little egg white or lemon juice until it flows, then use to flood the outlines. Burst any air bubbles that appear, then leave to dry.

6. When dry, pipe racket, strings, sails, etc., with white icing.

7. Using white icing and a piping bag fitted with a medium nozzle pipe two square outlines on the top of the cake about 2.5 cm/1 inch in from the cake's

edge. When dry, overpipe the inner square.

8. With the same nozzle pipe 'brackets' in each of the corners of the cake, making two lines of graduated lengths.

9. Midway between the brackets, along the sides, pipe five dots in a straight line. Then pipe three dots in front of these and finally two dots, one in front of the other in the centre.

10. Write the name on a piece of paper. Prick on to the cake and outline three times with white icing. When dry, overpipe and complete with dots. Leave to dry.

11. Using white icing and a thick writing nozzle, pipe a row of dots round the top edge of the cake. Pipe a second row on the side of the cake in between the first ones but so they just touch.

12. Pipe a row of large dots with a smaller one on top (by depressing the nozzle after piping the first part of the dot) all round the base of the cake.

13. Carefully stick a pair of bats and rackets or two boats on each side of the cake with a dab of icing. Leave to dry.

# RIBBON & ROSES CAKE

*Preparation time: icing and decorating the cake*

**For a one-tier cake:**

1 × 25 cm/10 inch square Rich Fruit Cake (page 11)

1 recipe quantity Apricot Glaze (page 27)

1 kg/2¼ lb Marzipan (page 22)

Royal Icing, made with 1.4 kg/3 lb icing sugar (page 24)

ribbon 1–2 cm/½–¾ inch wide

4 silver horseshoes

about 24 Icing Roses (page 44)

16 silver or white leaves (page 46)

This design is suitable for a one-, two- or three-tier cake, and makes a lovely birthday or wedding cake. For a three-tier cake, try 15 cm/6 inch, 20 cm/8 inch and 25 cm/10 inch tiers. The roses can be made of a pastel shade to match the ribbon; or it can be a white cake with white ribbon and pastel-coloured roses. If using colour on the cake, this colour can also be used with white flowers for the decoration on top of the cake.

1. Brush the top and sides of the cake with apricot glaze, then coat with marzipan (page 22). Leave to dry. Attach the cake to a 30 cm/12 inch silver cake board with a dab of icing.
2. Flat ice the cake, giving two or three coats all over and a further coat to the top, if necessary. Leave to dry for 24 hours.
3. Carefully lay the ribbon over the cake (as in the picture), attaching at the centre base of each side with a pin or dab of icing.
4. Using a medium writing nozzle and white icing, pipe three or four lines of graduated length on the sides of each cake in the 'V' between the ribbon. Add a dot at the end of each line and one under the shortest line.

5. Pipe a similar design on the top of the cake in the corners but on the inner side of the ribbon, graduating the lengths towards the centre of the cake.
6. Using a thick writing nozzle, pipe a border of dots around the top edge of the cake between the ribbon. Carry the dots down each corner of the cake and then round the base, making this border a little heavier.
7. Attach a horseshoe at the base of each corner of the cake.
8. On the sides of the cake, attach sprays of three roses and two leaves at the points of the ribbon, overlapping on to the board and on the top of the cake in the spaces between the ribbons. Leave to dry thoroughly.

# CHRISTENING CAKE FOR A BOY

*Preparation time: icing and decorating the cake*

1 × 20 cm/8 inch square Rich Fruit Cake (page 11)

1 recipe quantity Apricot Glaze (page 27)

800 g/1¾ lb Marzipan (page 22)

Royal Icing, made with 1.4 kg/3 lb icing sugar (page 24)

green or blue food colouring

little egg white, lightly beaten, or lemon juice, strained

silver balls

white and/or dark green or blue ribbon

1. Brush the top and sides of the cake with apricot glaze, then cover with marzipan (see page 22). Leave to dry. Attach the cake to a 25 cm/10 inch square silver cake board with a dab of icing.
2. Tint two-thirds of the icing pale green or blue with food colouring. Use to flat ice the cake, giving two coats all over and a third coat to the top if necessary (see pages 24 and 25). Leave to dry for 24 hours.
3. Draw a small train with two or three carriages, or trucks, on non-stick silicone paper so it will fit on the cake. Outline these using white icing and a medium writing nozzle. Leave to dry. Thin a little icing with egg white or lemon juice until it flows, then use to flood the train or trucks. Burst any bubbles which appear and leave until dry.
4. Write the child's name on a piece of paper and prick out on the cake. Make a double outline using white icing and a medium writing nozzle. When dry, overpipe and leave to dry. A row of tiny touching dots may also be piped on top of the outline of the name.
5. Position the train or trucks on the cake beneath the name and attach carefully with icing. Outline it all with white icing, adding windows, wheels, etc.
6. Pipe three straight lines in white icing in graduated lengths above the name and below the train, parallel to the edge of the cake. Pipe two small dots at the end of each line.
7. Using a fine star nozzle and white icing, pipe a zig-zag border all round the top edge of the cake.
8. Work another zig-zag on the side of the cake to join the first row and decorate the points with silver balls.
9. Work a heavier zig-zag border around the base of the cake, again decorating with silver balls. Leave to dry.
10. Tie the ribbon or ribbons round the side of the cake, with or without a bow.

# CHRISTENING CAKE FOR A GIRL

*Preparation time: icing and decorating the cake*

1 × 20 cm/8 inch round Rich Fruit Cake (page 11)

1 recipe quantity Apricot Glaze (page 27)

575 g/1¼ lb Marzipan (page 22)

Royal Icing, made with 900 g/2 lb icing sugar (page 24)

yellow food colouring

about 40 yellow Icing Roses (page 44)

yellow ribbon about 4 cm/ 1½ inches wide

1 baby's crib (see right)

A bought toy crib can be used to decorate the cake, or one can be made with a little imagination, using a matchbox and white lace. Or try using Gelatine or Moulding Icing (pages 20 and 21) to make the crib. Use about 50 g/2 oz white icing to mould the crib base, and about 25 g/1 oz white icing to form the hood for the crib. Attach the hood to the base with a dab of water. Make a small pillow of white icing and place in position. Tint about 25 g/1 oz icing a pale yellow and roll it out to make a cover; lay this over the base so it covers it completely and mark a criss-cross design on it. Leave to dry. If preferred the crib may be omitted altogether, and the name(s) written centrally on the cake.

1. Brush the top and sides of the cake with apricot glaze, then cover with marzipan (see page 22). Leave to dry. Attach the cake to a 25 cm/10 inch round silver cake board with a dab of icing.
2. Flat ice the cake, giving two coats all over and a third coat to the top if necessary (see pages 24 and 25). Leave to dry for 24 hours.
3. Make a template for an 8-point scallop (see page 37).
4. Tint about 2 tablespoons of the icing with yellow food colouring and put into a piping bag fitted with a medium writing nozzle.
5. Position the template on the cake and outline it using the yellow icing. Remove the template and pipe two more outlines, each a little inside the former. Leave to dry, then overpipe the centre line, again using yellow icing.
6. Write the name of the child on a piece of paper and prick out a little above the centre of the cake. Pipe with yellow icing; when dry overpipe and leave to dry again.
7. Using a fine star nozzle and white icing, pipe a continuous twisted edging to the top of the cake so it begins on the side of the cake and just overlaps on to the top.
8. Using a medium star nozzle and white icing, pipe another continuous twisted edging to the base of the cake to attach it to the board.
9. While the base border is still wet, attach a yellow rose to every alternate twist. Leave to dry.
10. Attach a yellow rose to each point of the scallops on the top of the cake.
11. Tie the ribbon round the sides of the cake, finishing with or without a bow.
12. Finally, attach the crib with a little icing so it stands inside the yellow outline just below the name.

# CONFIRMATION CAKE

*Preparation time: icing and decorating the cake*

1 × 23 cm/9 inch round Rich Fruit Cake (page 11)

1 recipe quantity Apricot Glaze (page 27)

800 g/1¾ lb Marzipan (page 22)

Royal Icing, made with 1.4 kg/3 lb icing sugar (page 24)

deep purple or other food colouring

9 white Icing Roses (page 44)

6 silver leaves

white or silver and white 4–5 cm/1½–2 inches wide ribbon

**FOR THE BIBLE:**

225 g/8 oz Marzipan (page 22)

deep red food colouring

1. Brush the top and sides of the cake with apricot glaze, then cover with marzipan (see page 22). Leave to dry. Attach the cake to a 28 cm/11 inch round silver cake board with a dab of icing.

2. Flat ice the cake, giving two coats all over and a third coat to the top if necessary (see pages 24 and 25). Leave to dry for 24 hours.

3. To make the Bible, knead the marzipan and shape into a rectangle. Place between sheets of polythene and roll out carefully into an open book shape, making a depression in the centre and at the ends as with an open book. This is done by pressing fairly firmly at each end, reducing the pressure until you come to the centre and then giving firm pressure in the centre again. Trim off the overhanging edges of the 'pages' and straighten the sides. Trim to give a border which represents the cover of the book. Make cuts into the sides of the book with a sharp knife to represent the pages.

4. Roll out the marzipan trimmings and cut into a cross to fit one of the pages; position on the left hand page and attach with a dab of icing. Using a fine paint brush and deep purple food colouring, paint the cross and the 'cover' of the book. Transfer the book to a sheet of greaseproof paper and leave in a warm place to dry. If necessary, add a second coat of colouring.

5. Make a hexagonal template (see page 37), making the points about 2.5 cm/1 inch from the edge of the cake. Using white icing and a medium writing nozzle, outline the hexagonal shape on top of the cake. Make two more outlines inside the first, leaving a small gap between them. Leave to dry, then overpipe the centre line.

6. Position the Bible a little above the centre of the hexagon and attach with icing. Using the writing nozzle, pipe words of your choice on the plain page of the book.

7. Write the name of the child on paper, then prick out on the cake in front of the Bible. Outline this in white icing and overpipe when dry.

8. In front of alternate sides of the hexagon write the initials of the child; in front of the other sides, arrange a spray of roses and silver leaves, attaching with icing.

9. Mark the top edges of the cake evenly into 12 or 18 portions, putting a small dot of icing on the cake and keeping it even with the lines of the hexagon on the top. Using a fine or medium star nozzle and white icing, pipe graduated twisted scrolls around the top edge of the cake between the dots (page 33) increasing pressure of icing in the centre of each scroll to make it larger and decreasing as you tail it off.

10. Work the same type of border round the base of the cake, making it a little heavier if preferred. Leave to dry.

11. Tie the ribbon round the side of the cake, with or without a bow.

# GOOD LUCK CAKE

*Preparation time: icing and decorating the cake*

1 × 20 cm/8 inch square Rich Fruit Cake (page 11)

1 recipe quantity Apricot Glaze (page 27)

800 g/1¾ lb Marzipan (page 22)

Royal Icing, made with 1.6 kg/ 3½ lb icing sugar (page 24)

blue food colouring

little egg white, lightly beaten, or lemon juice, strained

length of 2–2.5 cm/¾–1 inch wide ribbon

silver balls

1. Brush the top and sides of the cake with apricot glaze, then cover with marzipan (see page 22). Leave to dry. Attach the cake to a 25 cm/10 inch square silver cake board with a dab of icing.
2. Colour about three-quarters of the icing blue and use this to flat ice the cake, giving two coats all over and a third coat to top if necessary. Leave to dry for 24 hours.
3. On a piece of non-stick silicone paper write the words 'GOOD LUCK'.
4. Using a little white or coloured icing and a medium writing nozzle outline the words on the paper. Thin a little matching icing with egg white or lemon juice until it flows, then use to flood the letters. Burst any bubbles and leave to dry.
5. Place the ribbon over the cake as shown in the photograph and attach with icing.
6. Using a fine writing nozzle and contrasting icing, work rows of lattice on the cake between the ribbon and the corners, taking care to start and end each row of icing neatly as it acts as a border.
7. Position 'GOOD LUCK' on the cake and stick on with icing.
8. Using the medium writing nozzle and white icing, pipe sprays of lily of the valley on each side of the writing. This is done by piping slightly curved lines for both flowers and leaves and then adding dots to each side of some of the lines for the flowers.
9. Pipe two sprays of lily of the valley on each side of the cake in the same way.
10. Using a fine star or a rope or scroll nozzle, pipe a line of shells just inside the ribbons on top of the cake and along the edge of the cake where there is no lattice. Place a silver ball in between the shells on the lines across the top of the cake.
11. Pipe a heavier shell edging all round the base of the cake and down the corners. Leave to dry.

# 21st BIRTHDAY CAKE

*Preparation time: icing and decorating the cake*

---

1 × 20 cm/8 inch round Rich Fruit Cake (page 11)
1 recipe quantity Apricot Glaze (page 27)
575 g/1¼ lb Marzipan (page 22)
Royal Icing, made with 900 g/2 lb icing sugar (page 24)
little egg white, lightly beaten, or lemon juice, strained
mauve food colouring
60–70 mauve Icing Roses (page 44)
4 cm/1½ inches wide ribbon to match or tone with the flowers

The roses can be worked in two shades of the same colour, if preferred, e.g., pale and deeper pink. Two ribbons of different shades and widths may be used, one tied over the first.

1. Brush the top and sides of the cake with apricot glaze, then cover with marzipan (see page 22). Leave to dry. Attach the cake to a 25 cm/10 inch round silver cake board with a dab of icing.
2. Flat ice the cake, giving it two coats all over and a third coat on the top if necessary (see pages 24 and 25). Leave to dry for 24 hours.
3. Draw a '21' on non-stick silicone paper and outline in the same colour icing as the flowers, using a medium writing nozzle. Thin about 2 tablespoons of the same colour icing with a little egg white or lemon juice until it flows and place in a paper icing bag (page 29) without removing the tip. Cut off about 5 mm/¼ inch and fill in the numbers. Leave to dry.
4. Make an 8-point star template so that the points of the star come about 4 cm/1½ inches from the edge of the cake (see page 37). Place on the cake.
5. Using a medium writing nozzle and white icing, outline the template. Work a second row about 8 mm/⅓ inch inside this. When dry overpipe the outer line.
6. Using the contrasting colour icing and the medium writing nozzle, pipe small dots evenly between the two outlines of white icing. Leave to dry.
7. With the writing nozzle and white icing, work three 'V' shapes between the outer points of the star in graduated lengths.
8. Attach the '21' to the centre of the star with icing. An outline of the same colour icing can be worked on the numbers.
9. Using a fine star or rope or scroll nozzle and white icing, pipe a zig-zag from the top of the cake on to the side over the edge, keeping it neat and even-sized. Attach a rose to each point of the zig-zag both on the top and side of the cake.
10. Work another zig-zag border round the base of the cake. Attach roses to the lower points.
11. Tie the ribbon round the side of the cake and leave to dry.

# HORSESHOE ENGAGEMENT CAKE

*Preparation time: icing and decorating
the cake*

1 × 23–25 cm/9–10 inch round
 Rich Fruit Cake (page 11), cut to
 a horseshoe shape (see page 35)
1 recipe quantity Apricot Glaze
 (page 27)
800 g/1¾ lb Marzipan (page 22)
Royal Icing, made with 1.75 kg/
 4 lb icing sugar (page 24)
food colouring (optional)
about 100 coloured Icing Roses
 (page 44)
little egg white, lightly beaten, or
 lemon juice, strained
about 4 white Butterfly Run-outs
 (page 53)

The number of roses required depends on the size of the cake. If preferred a mixture of coloured and white flowers can be used with any corresponding decorations the same colour as the roses.

1. Brush the top and sides of the cake with apricot glaze, then cover with marzipan (see page 22). Leave to dry. Attach the cake to a round silver cake board about 5 cm/2 inches larger than the cake with a dab of icing.
2. Using white or coloured icing, flat ice the cake, giving two coats all over and a third coat to the top if necessary (see pages 24 and 25). Leave to dry for 24 hours.

3. Put about 5 tablespoons white icing into a piping bag fitted with a medium writing nozzle.
4. Draw two heart shapes on non-stick silicone paper and outline these with white icing. Leave to dry.
5. Thin the remaining white icing with a little egg white or lemon juice until it flows, then use to flood the hearts. Burst any air bubbles with a pin and leave to dry for 24 hours. If in doubt of breakages, make a third heart.
6. Write the required names on pieces of paper. Position evenly on the cake on each side of the centre front of the horseshoe and prick out carefully.
7. Put some white icing into a piping bag fitted with a medium nozzle and outline the names. When dry, overpipe with the white icing using the writing nozzle.
8. With coloured icing, outline the hearts with one or two rows of small dots.
9. Using a thick writing nozzle and white or coloured icing, pipe a row of plain dots all round the top edge of the cake and another of larger dots all round the base of the cake to attach it to the board. Leave to dry.
10. Using the coloured icing and medium nozzle, work a shallow scallop around the side of the cake joining each alternate dot from the top edge of the cake.
11. Attach the butterflies, and attach the two hearts to the top of the cake, using icing.
12. Finally, attach roses all round the sides of the cake to give a scalloped effect. To keep these even a curved template can be used and moved round the cake as you attach the flowers. The inside of the horseshoe can be left plain if there are insufficient roses but it will look better with them. Leave to dry.

# ELIZA WEDDING CAKE

*Preparation time: icing and decorating the cake*

**For a two-tier cake**

1 × 15 cm/6 inch square and 1 × 25 cm/10 inch square Rich Fruit Cake (page 11)

2 recipe quantities Apricot Glaze (page 27)

1½ kg/3¼ lb Marzipan (page 22)

Royal Icing, made with 1.75 kg/4 lb icing sugar (page 24)

1 recipe quantity Moulding or Gelatine icing (page 20–21)

pink and green food colouring

This design is suitable for a one-, two- or three-tier cake. The oval plaques and roses can be made of the same colour or, if preferred, two different pastel shades.

1. Brush the top and sides of the cakes with apricot glaze, then cover with marzipan (see page 22). Leave to dry. Attach the smaller cake to a 20 cm/8 inch square silver cake board with a dab of icing, and the larger cake to a 30 cm/12 inch cake board.
2. Flat ice the cakes, giving three coats all over and an extra coat to the tops of the cakes if necessary (see pages 24 and 25). Leave to dry for 24 hours.
3. Tint three-quarters of the gelatine or moulding icing a very pale pink. Use half of this icing to mould 24 roses, 12 of which are smaller than the others (see page 50). Leave to dry.
4. Roll out the remaining pink icing thinly and cut into four oval shapes with straight sides, about 5 × 4 cm/2 × 1½ inches, and four ovals 10 × 5 cm/4 × 2 inches. Place on greaseproof or non-stick silicone paper and leave to dry for 24 hours.
5. Roll out the remaining white gelatine or moulding icing and use to make 40 small rose-shaped leaves.
6. Make an Eliza template (see page 37) and position on the smaller cake. Using a medium writing nozzle and white icing, outline it. Work a second outline just inside the first.
7. Work two graduated length lines outside the straight edges of the outline. Repeat on the larger cake.
8. On the sides of the cakes, pipe double curved lines to form half a diamond from each corner.
9. Attach the icing ovals to the sides of the cakes with icing – the larger ovals on the large cake – and leave to dry.
10. Using a fine star nozzle and white icing work a shell or twisted shell edging to the top edge of each cake.
11. Work a heavier border round the bases using a fine or medium star nozzle.
12. Work dots or a shell design round each of the ovals, a little in from the edge using the smaller star nozzle.
13. Attach a rose and two leaves to each of the spaces in the corners on top of the cakes and another rose and two leaves at the points of the curved diamonds on the sides of the cakes. Use the smaller roses for the smaller cake.
14. Assemble the cake tiers with four square pillars and top with a vase of fresh flowers.

# HILARY WEDDING CAKE

*Preparation time: icing and decorating the cake*

**For a three-tier cake:**

1 × 13 cm/5 inch square, 1 × 20 cm/8 inch square and 1 × 28 cm/11 inch square Rich Fruit Cake (page 11)

3 recipe quantities Apricot Glaze (page 27)

2.25 kg/5 lb Marzipan (page 22)

Royal Icing, made with 3.5 kg/8 lb icing sugar (page 34)

about 40 white or pastel Icing Roses (page 44)

about 24 silver leaves or Icing Leaves (page 46)

This design is suitable for a one-, two- or three-tier cake, and can be adapted to fit a round cake, if preferred.

1. Brush the top and sides of the cakes with apricot glaze, then cover with marzipan (see page 22). Leave to dry. Attach the cakes to square silver cake boards, 18 cm/7 inch, 25 cm/10 inch and 35 cm/14 inch, with dabs of icing.
2. Flat ice the cakes, giving three coats all over and an extra coat to the tops of the cakes if necessary (see pages 24 and 25). Leave to dry for 24 hours.
3. Make templates for the tops of the cakes (see pages 36 and 37) in graduated sizes and another for the sides of the cakes, using a pair of compasses to keep them even.
4. Position the template on the top of each cake and outline using white icing and a medium writing nozzle. Leave to dry, then pipe a second row just inside the first one.
5. Using either the same writing nozzle or a finer one, work a lace pattern between the outlines of icing, taking it carefully over the edges of the cakes. Leave to dry.
7. Using a thick writing nozzle, pipe a border of large dots round the base of each cake to attach to the board.
8. Using the same nozzle pipe a slightly smaller dot in front of each of the first ones, this time on the cake board.
9. A little icing can be tinted to match the roses and, using a medium nozzle, the inner outline on top of the cakes and lower outline on the sides can be overpiped with it; otherwise overpipe in white.
10. Attach roses and leaves to the cakes as in the photograph, using a little icing. On the largest cake, two or three roses can be added in some of these places.
11. Assemble the cake tiers using four pillars on each tier and decorate the top of the cake with an arrangement of fresh flowers in a vase or a low arrangement to match the bride's bouquet.

**Back: Hilary wedding cake**
**Front: Eliza wedding cake**

# FLEUR WEDDING CAKE

*Preparation time: icing and decorating the cake*

**For a three-tier cake:**

1 × 15 cm/6 inch round, 1 × 20 cm/8 inch round and 1 × 25 cm/10 inch round Rich Fruit Cake (page 11)

3 recipe quantities Apricot Glaze (page 27)

1.75 kg/4 lb Marzipan (page 22)

Royal Icing, made with 3 kg/7 lb icing sugar (page 24)

about 70 white Icing Roses (page 44)

about 120 very pale coloured icing Roses (page 44)

about 140 slightly darker Icing Roses (page 44)

18 silver or Icing Leaves (page 46)

This design is suitable for a one-, two- or three-tier cake.

1. Brush the top and sides of the cakes with apricot glaze, then coat with marzipan (see page 22). Leave to dry. Attach the cakes to round silver cake boards, 20 cm/8 inch, 25 cm/10 inch and 33 cm/13 inch, with a dab of icing.
2. Flat ice the cakes, giving three coats all over and an extra coat to the tops of the cakes if necessary (see pages 24 and 25). Leave to dry for 24 hours.
3. Make six-point curved templates (page 37) to fit the tops of the cakes.
4. Position a template on each cake and outline in white icing using a medium writing nozzle.
5. Fill in to the edge of each cake with three rows of curved lattice in white, beginning by piping lines parallel to the outline curve but about 8 mm/⅓ inch apart.
6. Pipe an outline inside the trellis on the tops of the cakes in white.
7. Tint a little icing to match the roses, and using this and a medium writing nozzle overpipe the white outlines.
8. Mark the six points on the sides of the

cakes, midway between the curves worked on the top, with a white rose. This is the beginning of the garlands of roses.
9. Using a template or freehand, attach roses to fit the curves, running through the sides from white to the darkest colour in the centre – i.e. at the bottom of the curve, and continuing all round the sides of the cakes. Add leaves at intervals.
10. With a fine star or rope or scroll nozzle, pipe a shell border to the top edge of each cake, taking the tip of each alternate shell on to the top of the cake.
11. Using a slightly thicker nozzle, work a similar design border around the base of each cake, taking the tips of the shells on to the sides of the cakes and the board. Leave to dry.
12. On the smallest cake tier place a white or palest colour rose at the tip of the point of the trellis on the top of the cake. On the middle tier add a white and palest colour rose, and on the large tier add one of each colour at each point.
13. Assemble the cake tiers using four round pillars on the bottom tier and three or four on the middle tier. Top with a flower decoration.

# LAURA WEDDING CAKE

*Preparation time: icing and decorating the cakes*

**For a two-tier cake:**
1 × 25 cm/10 inch round and
   1 × 15 or 18 cm/6 or 7 inch
   round Rich Fruit Cake (page 11)
2 recipe quantities Apricot Glaze
   (page 27)
1.4 kg/3 lb Marzipan (page 22)
Royal Icing, made with 1.6 kg/
   3½ lb icing sugar (page 24)
yellow or orange food colouring
about 72 Icing Narcissi (page 45)
24 white Icing Leaves (page 46)

This design is suitable for a one-, two- or three-tier cake. White or coloured roses or other flowers may be used in place of narcissi.

1.  Brush the top and sides of the cakes with apricot glaze, then cover with the marzipan (see page 22). Leave to dry. Attach the cakes to round silver cake boards 33 cm/13 inch and 20 or 23 cm/8 or 9 inch, with a dab of icing.
2.  Flat ice the cakes, giving three coats all over and an extra coat to the tops of the cakes if necessary (see pages 24 and 25). Leave to dry for 24 hours.
3.  Make the Laura templates to fit the tops of the cakes (see page 37).
4.  Outline the templates on the cakes using a medium writing nozzle and white icing.
5.  Work lines inside the first all the way to the edge of the cakes, keeping the lines about 8 mm/⅓ inch apart.
6.  Tint a little icing either the yellow or orange of the narcissi and put into a piping bag fitted with a medium writing nozzle. Pipe a row of dots just inside the outline on the top of the cakes.
7.  A row of dots can be piped using the same nozzle and coloured icing, all round the sides of the cakes about 1 cm/½ inch from the edge, dipping the row down into a point under the gaps on top of the cakes as in the photograph.
8.  Using a thick writing nozzle and white icing, pipe a continuous, even, twisted edging to the top of the cakes.
9.  With the same or a larger writing nozzle, pipe a continuous twisted edging round the bases but making each third twist larger than the previous two.
10.  Attach one leaf and three to five narcissi (depending on the size of the cake) to the spaces on the top of the cakes between the lines; the leaf should protrude well over the edge.
11.  Attach one flower and two leaves under the centre of the piped lines high on the sides of the cakes and three to six lower down under the flowers on top of the cakes.
12.  To complete the decoration, pipe 'ribbons' or streamers from the single flower to link with the others. Overpipe when dry.
13.  Assemble the cake tiers using four round pillars. Top with a flower decoration.

# DAISY SILVER WEDDING CAKE

*Preparation time: icing and decorating the cake*

1 × 20 or 23 cm/8 or 9 inch square Rich Fruit Cake (page 11)
1 recipe quantity Apricot Glaze (page 27)
800–900 g/1¾–2 lb Marzipan (page 22)
Royal Icing, made with 1.25 kg/2½ lb icing sugar (page 24)
about 80 silver balls
8 medium silver horseshoes

This design can also be used for a tiered wedding cake if you omit '25's' and horseshoes from the top of the cake. The smallest tier will only need one daisy at the points of the lattice on the top tier and one at the points of the diamond lattice on the sides. The larger tier or tiers will take more daisies, especially on the sides. Also use graduated sizes of silver horseshoes. The Marzipan and Royal Icing tables on pages 22 and 24 will serve as a guide to quantities, but allow extra for decoration.

1. Brush the top and sides of the cake with apricot glaze then cover with marzipan (see page 22). Leave to dry. Attach the cake to a 25 or 28 cm/10 or 11 inch square silver cake board with a dab of icing.

2. Flat ice the cake, giving it two coats all over and a third coat to the top if necessary (see pages 24 and 25). Leave to dry for 24 hours.
3. To make the daisies, using a petal nozzle pipe out six flat and fairly spiky petals all from the centre of the flower on a small square of non-stick silicone paper. Complete by placing a silver ball in the centre. Repeat to make 100 daisies. Leave to dry.
4. Mark a square on top of the cake with the points coming to the centre of each side edge. Outline in icing using a medium writing nozzle. Pipe a second square about 8 mm/⅓ inch inside the first one.
5. Make a square template to fit inside the marked outline, again with the points coming to the centre of each side edge, i.e. the same way as the shape of the cake. Outline with the writing nozzle; remove the template.
6. Fill in the triangles formed with a lattice as follows. First pipe horizontal lines about 8 mm/⅓ inch apart parallel to the centre outline and leave to dry. Then turn the cake and pipe across these lines at right angles, again at 8 mm/⅓ inch intervals. Leave to dry. Finally pipe a third row over the first line of the lattice.
7. With the same nozzle pipe a line of small dots between the icing outlines to the lattice.
8. Make diamond shape templates of two sizes to fit the sides of the cake – the centre one should be large enough to reach from the top edge of the cake to the board; the other should be rather smaller. Prick out on to each side.
9. Using the writing nozzle outline the diamonds, then work a lattice to fill each one. Work three rows, allowing each to dry before adding the next layer.
10. In each corner of the cake top mark a '25' and pipe in white icing; overpipe when dry.
11. Using a thick writing nozzle pipe a base border of large plain dots all round the cake; attach a horseshoe at each corner.
12. Attach four horseshoes in the centre of the cake using large dots of icing and making them stand up to face the sides of the cake.
13. Attach one daisy at each end of the small diamonds of lattice on the sides of the cake and one or two between the large and small diamonds.
14. Finally attach daisies all round the top edge of the cake to form a border.

# GOLDEN WEDDING CAKE

*Preparation time: icing and decorating the cake*

1 × 25 cm/10 inch square Rich Fruit Cake (page 11)
1 recipe quantity Apricot Glaze (page 27)
1 kg/2¼ lb Marzipan (page 22)
Royal Icing, made with 1.4 kg/3 lb icing sugar (page 24)
little egg white, lightly beaten, or lemon juice, strained
yellow food colouring
gold 'silver' balls
36–40 Christmas Roses with gold ball instead of iced centres (page 45)
8 gold leaves
8 gold horseshoes

1. To make the cake octagonal, make marks along the sides of the cake 7 cm/2¾ inches from each end. Cut off each corner. The sides should each measure 10 cm/4 inches.

2. Brush the top and sides of the cake with apricot glaze, then cover with marzipan (see page 22). Leave to dry. Attach the cake to a cake board with a dab of icing.

3. Flat ice the cake, giving it two coats all over. To do the sides, ice four alternate sections and then when dry ice the other four. Add a third coat of icing to the top if necessary (see pages 24 and 25). Leave to dry for 24 hours.

4. Draw a '50' and 'YEARS' on non-stick silicone paper, making the numbers about 4 cm/1½ inches tall and the letters much smaller. Using white icing and a medium writing nozzle outline the numbers and letters. Thin a little icing with egg white or lemon juice until it flows, then use to flood the numbers and letters. Burst any bubbles that appear. Leave to dry.

5. Prick out 'CONGRATULATIONS' on the top of the cake and outline it. When dry, overpipe.

6. Tint a little icing yellow (to represent gold) and use to outline an octagonal on top of the cake as shown. Pipe a second line just inside the first.

7. Using a scroll or rope nozzle and white icing pipe a border of two graduated scrolls round the top edge of the cake and another similar border round the base.

8. Attach gold balls down the centre of the '50'. Attach the numbers to the centre of the cake with icing, making them stand up if preferred. Position 'YEARS' just in front and attach.

9. Arrange three or four roses and two gold leaves on top of the cake beside alternate outlines and attach with icing.

10. On alternate sides attach two overlapping gold horseshoes.

11. On the remaining sides arrange a circle of roses and attach with icing. Leave to dry.

# EASTER & CHRISTMAS CAKES

Religious festivals are celebrated throughout the world and a special cake is usually part of the festivities. Although the type of cake varies from country to country and for the different festivals, we tend to celebrate the two main festivals of Christmas and Easter with splendid rich cakes topped by plenty of marzipan and icing and elegant, simple or novel decorations.

Christmas cakes can be made several weeks before required to help ease the inevitable cooking involved in the holiday period. They should be stored with their greaseproof paper and in an airtight container or wrapped in foil.

Marzipan can be added 2–3 weeks before the day, and once dry (allow about 5–7 days) the icing can be completed and decorations added so the cake is finished well in time. It is preferable to allow a flat iced cake to dry for 24 hours before beginning the decorating. Store it in a dry place, uncovered except, perhaps, for a sheet of greaseproof paper laid loosely over the top. If you put the cake into a tin or closed container the oils from the cake and marzipan may seep through into the icing and discolour it more quickly than usual. The flowers, leaves and other decorations for the cake can be made well in advance because both marzipan and icing models and flowers keep well for several months.

The popular cake for Easter is the delicious Simnel cake. The marzipan layer baked in the centre makes the cake very moist and flavoursome. Again the cake can be made about 10 days beforehand and stored, wrapped in foil, until it is decorated a few days before Easter.

Not everyone likes a fruit cake so there are celebration cakes in this section with a sponge base, such cakes as the Yule Log, Santa's Stocking and Easter Bunny Cake.

Some of the models and decorations used for the following designs appear in the recipes, but most are in the chapter on Special Decorations (pages 44–53). For piping techniques see pages 31–34.

# SIMNEL CAKE

*Preparation time: about 40 minutes,*
*    plus decorating*
*Cooking time: about 2 hours*
*Oven: 160°C, 325°F, Gas Mark 3*

200 g/8 oz plain flour
pinch of salt
1 teaspoon baking powder
1 teaspoon ground cinnamon
pinch of ground nutmeg
150 g/6 oz butter
150 g/6 oz soft brown sugar
3 eggs (sizes 1, 2)
2 tablespoons milk
100 g/4 oz seedless raisins
150 g/6 oz currants
100 g/4 oz sultanas
50 g/2 oz chopped mixed peel
50 g/2 oz glacé cherries, quartered,
    washed and dried
grated rind of 1 orange
1 recipe quantity Marzipan
    (page 22)
little apricot jam or egg white

DECORATION:
fluffy chickens or rabbits
yellow ribbon

This Easter cake has a layer of marzipan baked in the centre of it. Sometimes the marzipan topping is lightly toasted before the decoration is added. Simply place the cake under a moderate grill for 1–2 minutes, turning the cake and watching all the time, until the top is lightly browned.

1.  Sift together the flour, salt, baking powder, cinnamon and nutmeg.
2.  Cream the butter and sugar together until light and fluffy.
3.  Beat the eggs into the creamed mixture one at a time, following each with a spoonful of the flour mixture. Fold in the remainder of the flour alternately with the milk.
4.  Combine the dried fruits, peel, cherries and orange rind and stir into the mixture. Spread half the mixture in a greased and lined 18 cm/7 inch round deep cake tin.
5.  Roll out one-third of the marzipan and trim to an 18 cm/7 inch round to fit the cake tin. Lay on the cake mixture in the tin, then cover with the remainder of the cake mixture.

6.  Bake in a preheated oven for about 2 hours or until cooked through and the sides of the cake have shrunk slightly from the tin. Cool in the tin for 10 minutes, then turn on to a wire rack and cool completely.
7.  Roll out just over half of the remaining marzipan to a round to fit the top of the cake.
8.  Brush the top of the cake with jam or egg white and place the marzipan round in position. Mark a criss-cross pattern on the round with a sharp knife and decorate the edge.
9.  Roll the rest of the marzipan into 11 even-sized balls and arrange around the edge of the marzipan round, attaching each with a dab of jam or egg white.
10.  Position the chickens or rabbits in the centre of the cake and tie a ribbon round the outside.

# EASTER FRUIT CAKE

*Preparation time: about 45 minutes,*
*    plus icing and decorating*
*Cooking time: 2–2½ hours*
*Oven: 160°C, 325°F, Gas Mark 3*

275 g/10 oz currants
150 g/5 oz sultanas
150 g/5 oz seedless raisins
50 g/2 oz chopped mixed peel
grated rind of 1 orange
grated rind of 1 lemon
225 g/8 oz plain flour
pinch of salt
1 teaspoon ground cinnamon
¾ teaspoon ground nutmeg
150 g/6 oz butter or margarine
150 g/6 oz caster or light soft
    brown sugar
3 eggs (sizes 1, 2)
2 tablespoons orange or lemon
    juice
175–225 g/6–8 oz Marzipan
    (page 22)
little jam or egg white
Royal Icing made with 225 g/8 oz
    icing sugar (page 24)
little lemon juice
8–12 tiny foil-covered chocolate
    Easter eggs
3 or 4 marzipan daffodils and
    leaves (page 52)
yellow and/or orange ribbon

A not-so-traditional Easter cake, this is for those who prefer a layer of icing on a fruit cake. Alternatively, decorate the cake like the traditional Simnel Cake (above).

1.  Combine the dried fruits, peel and orange and lemon rinds.
2.  Sift the flour with the salt and spices.
3.  Cream the butter or margarine with the sugar until light and fluffy.
4.  Beat in the eggs one at a time, following each with a spoonful of the flour. Fold in the rest of the flour, then stir in the dried fruit mixture and the orange or lemon juice.
5.  Turn into a greased and lined 18 cm/7 inch square cake tin and level the top. Bake in a preheated oven for 2–2¼ hours or until a skewer inserted into the centre of the cake comes out clean.
6.  Cool in the tin, then turn on to a wire rack.
7.  Roll out the marzipan thinly to a square to fit the top of the cake. Brush the top of the cake with a little jam or egg white and place the marzipan square in position. Leave to dry.
8.  Tie a piece of double-thickness foil or greaseproof paper tightly round the sides of the cake to come at least 2.5 cm/1 inch above the top of the cake.

9.  Put a small amount of royal icing in an icing bag fitted with a medium star nozzle. thin the rest of the icing slightly with lemon juice or lightly beaten egg white so it just flows, then pour over the top of the cake. Allow the icing to run out to the edges to touch the paper, using a palette knife to spread it, if necessary. As the icing settles burst any air bubbles with a pin. Leave to set.
10.  Remove the foil or paper from the cake. Arrange the chocolate eggs around the top edge of the cake on the icing and the marzipan daffodils and leaves in the centre. Using the star nozzle, pipe a shell border on the edge of the icing. Complete by tying the ribbon into a bow round the sides of the cake.

*From the left: Easter fruit cake;*
*Simnel cake*

# EASTER EGG CAKE

*Preparation time: about 30 minutes
 plus icing and decorating*
*Cooking time: about 45 minutes*
*Oven: 160°C, 325°F, Gas Mark 3*

3-egg chocolate Quick Mix Cake
 mixture (page 12)
1½ recipe quantities chocolate
 Butter Cream (page 26)
red, yellow or green ribbon
selection of Marzipan Flowers
 (page 50), e.g. daffodils, violets,
 and Marzipan leaves (page 52)

To make the smaller Easter egg use a 2-egg cake mixture and smaller dishes.

1.  Divide the cake mixture between two greased and floured oval 600 ml/1 pint ovenproof glass dishes.
2.  Bake in a preheated oven for about 45 minutes or until well risen and firm to the touch. Turn on to a wire rack and leave to cool.
3.  Use a little of the butter cream to sandwich the cakes together to give an egg shape. Stand the cake on a cake board.
4.  Use the remaining butter cream to mask the whole cake. Smooth the surface with a palette knife.

5.  Cut a strip of greaseproof paper the same width as the ribbon and lay across the cake, moulding it round as if the cake were tied up. Place the ribbon over the greaseproof paper. If preferred, complete with a ribbon bow on the side.
6.  Arrange a spray of marzipan flowers and leaves on each side of the ribbon, attaching them to the butter cream. Leave to set.

**VARIATIONS:**
The cake may be flavoured vanilla, coffee or any other flavour, if preferred, or a Madeira Cake mixture (page 16) may be used.

# EASTER BUNNY CAKE

*Preparation time: 40 minutes,
    plus decorating*
*Cooking time: about 50 minutes*
*Oven: 160°C, 325°F, Gas Mark 3*

5-egg Quick Mix Cake mixture
    (page 12) in any flavour
1 recipe quantity Apricot Glaze
    (page 27)
1½ recipe quantities vanilla Butter
    Cream (page 26)
pink food colouring
2 chocolate buttons or beans
3 chocolate matchsticks

1. Put the 5-egg cake mixture in a
30 × 25 × 5 cm/12 × 10 × 2 inch roasting tin
lined with greased greaseproof paper.
Level the top, making sure the corners are
well filled.
2. Bake in a preheated oven for about 50
minutes or until well risen and firm to the
touch. Turn on to a wire rack and leave
until cold. Place the cake upside-down on
a cake board.
3. Cut a piece of greaseproof paper the
same size as the cake and draw a rabbit
shape and separate tail on it.
4. Cut out the pattern, place on the cake
and carefully cut the cake to the same
shapes with a sharp pointed knife.

Position the tail on the rabbit's body.
5. Brush the cake all over with apricot
glaze.
6. Put a small amount of butter cream in a
piping bag fitted with a medium star
nozzle and use to pipe stars all over the
rabbit's tail and inside his ears.
7. Tint the rest of the butter cream pink (or
yellow, if preferred), put into another
piping bag fitted with a medium star
nozzle and pipe stars all over the body
including the sides of the cake, making
sure each star touches the ones next to it.
8. Position a chocolate button or bean for
the bunny's nose and another for his eye.
Add the chocolate matchsticks for his
whiskers. Leave to set.

# CHRISTMAS CAKE

*Preparation time: about 20 minutes*
*Cooking time: 3½–3¾ hours*
*Oven: 150°C, 300°F, Gas Mark 2*

225 g/8 oz seedless raisins
225 g/8 oz currants
225 g/8 oz sultanas
100 g/4 oz chopped mixed peel
50 g/2 oz almonds, ground or
    finely chopped
50 g/2 oz glacé cherries, quartered,
    washed and dried
grated rind of 1 lemon
225 g/8 oz butter
175 g/6 oz light or dark soft brown
    sugar
4 eggs (sizes 1, 2)
225 g/8 oz plain flour
pinch of salt
1 teaspoon mixed spice
½ teaspoon ground cinnamon
good pinch of ground nutmeg
2 tablespoons brandy, sherry or
    lemon juice
3–4 tablespoons brandy (optional)

1. Mix together the dried fruits, peel, almonds, cherries and lemon rind.
2. Cream the butter and sugar together until light and creamy.
3. Beat in the eggs one at a time following each with a tablespoon of the flour.
4. Sift the remaining flour with the salt and spices and fold into the creamed mixture followed by the brandy, sherry or lemon juice. Add the fruit mixture and combine well.
5. Turn into a greased and lined 20 cm/8 inch round or 18 cm/7 inch square cake tin, level the top, then make a slight hollow in the centre.
6. Wrap several thicknesses of brown paper or newspaper round the outside of the tin and bake in a preheated oven for 3½–3¾ hours or until a skewer inserted into the centre of the cake comes out clean.
7. Cool in the tin, then turn out on to a wire rack. Store in an airtight container or wrapped in foil until required.
8. If using extra brandy, pierce the cake all over with a fine skewer and drizzle 3–4 tablespoons brandy over it before storing.

**From the back: Father Christmas & reindeer cake;**
**Economical fruit cake; Christmas cake**

# ECONOMICAL FRUIT CAKE

**VARIATIONS:**
For larger Christmas cakes, use 1½ quantities of the mixture and bake in a 23 cm/9 inch round or 20 cm/8 inch square cake tin, allowing 4–4½ hours.
Use double quantity of the mixture for a 25 cm/10 inch round or 23 cm/9 inch square cake tin and allow 4½–5 hours baking.

*Preparation time: about 20 minutes*
*Cooking time: about 2½ hours*
*Oven: 160°C, 325°F, Gas Mark 3*

50–100 g/2–4 oz glacé cherries, quartered, washed and dried
175 g/6 oz currants
175 g/6 oz sultanas
50 g/2 oz ground almonds
50–100 g/2–4 oz chopped mixed peel
225 g/8 oz soft (tub) margarine
225 g/8 oz caster or light soft brown sugar
4 eggs, beaten
225 g/8 oz plain flour
1 teaspoon mixed spice
grated rind of 1 orange or lemon
2 tablespoons orange or lemon juice
2 tablespoons milk

This recipe makes a fairly deep cake. If you prefer a shallower cake, bake the mixture in a 23 cm/9 inch round or 20 cm/8 inch square cake tin. This cake is best kept for just a week before eating. It can be covered with Marzipan (page 22) and Royal Icing (page 24) as any Christmas cake, but don't make it too long before Christmas.

1. Mix together the cherries, currants, sultanas, ground almonds and peel.
2. Cream the margarine and sugar together until light and creamy.
3. Beat in the eggs one at a time following each with a tablespoon of the flour.
4. Sift the remaining flour with the mixed spice and fold into the creamed mixture with the orange or lemon rind followed by the orange or lemon juice and milk. Add the fruit mixture and combine well.
5. Turn into a greased and lined 20 cm/8 inch round or 18 cm/7 inch square cake tin and level the top.
6. Bake in a preheated oven for about 2½ hours or until well risen and firm to the touch, and a skewer inserted into the centre comes out clean.
7. Cool in the tin, then turn out on to a wire rack. Store in an airtight container, or wrapped in foil, until required.

# FATHER CHRISTMAS & REINDEER CAKE

*Preparation time: icing and decorating the cake*

1 × 20 cm/8 inch round Christmas Cake (see left), or Economical Fruit Cake (see above)
1 recipe quantity Apricot Glaze (page 27)
575 g/1¼ lb Marzipan (page 22)
Royal Icing made with 675 g/1½ lb icing sugar (page 24)

**DECORATION:**
1 Marzipan Father Christmas (page 49)
1 Marzipan Reindeer and Sledge (pages 48 and 49)
9 Marzipan Holly Leaves and Berries (page 52)
red or green ribbon

1. Brush the top and sides of the cake with apricot glaze, then cover with marzipan (see page 22). Leave to dry. Attach the cake to a silver cake board with a dab of icing.
2. Make up the icing a little stiffer than usual. Completely mask the cake roughly with the icing.
3. Make sure there is a flat strip all round the side of the cake for the ribbon, then with a spoon handle or small palette knife, pull the icing up into peaks all over. Extra icing can be added with the spoon if necessary.
4. Leave to dry slightly, then position the Father Christmas, sledge and reindeer.
5. Complete the decoration with three sets of three marzipan holly leaves and berries.
6. When completely dry, tie the ribbon round the cake, finishing with, or without, a bow.

# MERRY CHRISTMAS CAKE

*Preparation time: icing and decorating the cake*

1 × 18 cm/7 inch or 20 cm/8 inch square Christmas Cake (page 74)

1 recipe quantity Apricot Glaze (page 27)

800 g/1¾ lb Marzipan (page 22)

Royal Icing made with 900 g/2 lb icing sugar (page 24)

**DECORATIONS:**

red and brown food colourings

2 silver balls

about 30 Marzipan Holly Leaves and Berries (page 52)

1. Brush the top and sides of the cake with apricot glaze, then cover with marzipan (see page 22), reserving about 100 g/4 oz for the decoration. Leave to dry. Attach the cake to a silver cake board with a dab of icing.
2. Flat ice the cake all over giving it two coats (see pages 24 and 25). Leave to dry.
3. To make the robin for the decoration, use 15 g/½ oz of the reserved marzipan. Colour a small piece of it red and the remainder brown. Mould two small flat pieces for wings and mark feathers with a knife. Mould the remainder into a bird shape with head and pointed beak, and a tail. Use red marzipan to mould over the robin's breast, up to his beak. Attach the wings, mark the tail feathers with a knife and add two silver balls for the eyes. Leave to dry.
4. Roll out about 50 g/2 oz of the remaining marzipan and cut to a rectangle about 12.5 × 7.5 cm/5 × 3 inches. Position on the cake across the centre; attach with icing.
5. Using white icing and a medium writing nozzle, pipe the words 'MERRY CHRISTMAS' on the plaque. Pipe one or two outlines on to the cake to surround the plaque.

6. Colour the remaining marzipan red with food colouring. Roll out thinly and use to make a small lantern. Attach to the plaque together with the robin, using a dab of icing.
7. Pipe three lines of 'corners' on the cake, making each a little shorter than the last one, using the medium writing nozzle. Add dots to alternate corners as shown.
8. Attach a set of three holly leaves with berries to the corners without the dots.
9. Arrange a continuous border of holly leaves and berries around the side of the cake, attaching each with a little icing.
10. Using a medium star nozzle, pipe a sloping shell edging around the top edge of the cake, with each shell beginning on the top of the cake and ending on the side.
11. Use a thicker star nozzle to pipe a shell border around the base to seal the cake to the board. Leave to set.

# HOLLY & IVY CHRISTMAS CAKE

*Preparation time: icing and decorating the cake*

1 × 18 cm/7 inch or 20 cm/8 inch square or round, Christmas Cake (page 74)

1 recipe quantity Apricot Glaze (page 27)

675 g/1½ lb Marzipan (page 22)

Royal Icing made with 900 g/2 lb icing sugar (page 24)

little lemon juice or beaten egg white

**DECORATION:**

5 Christmas Roses (page 45)

4 Marzipan Ivy Leaves (page 52)

12 Marzipan Holly Leaves and Berries (page 52)

This design can be used for a round or square cake; with a square cake, arrange the points of the cross to come to the corners of the cake. Four Robins (see Merry Christmas Cake, above) can also be put on the top of the cake, with a dab of icing.

1. Brush the top and sides of the cake with apricot glaze, then cover with marzipan (see page 22). Leave to dry. Attach the cake to a silver cake board with a dab of icing.
2. Flat ice the top of the cake only (see pages 24 and 25), giving it two coats. Leave to dry.
3. Draw a cross shape on a piece of paper the same size as the top of the cake, making the cross about 3 cm/1¼ inches wide. Cut out and place on top of the cake.
4. Using a piping bag fitted with a medium writing nozzle, outline the cross with royal icing. Remove the paper pattern and leave to dry.
5. Thin a little of the royal icing with lightly beaten egg white or strained lemon juice until it just flows, then spoon inside the lines of icing to fill the cross

completely. Burst any air bubbles which appear with a pin. Leave to set.
6. Thicken the rest of the icing slightly with extra icing sugar, then use most of it to rough ice the sides of the cake. Pull the icing up into peaks all over, using a spoon handle or small palette knife. Let the peaks of icing just overlap on to the top of the cake to give it an edging.
7. Put the remaining icing into a piping bag fitted with a small star nozzle and pipe a narrow line of stars or shells to outline the cross.
8. Arrange a bunch of Christmas roses and ivy leaves in the centre of the cross, and holly leaves and berries along the spokes of the cross. Attach the decorations to the cake with a little icing. Leave to dry.

**Back: Merry Christmas cake;**
**Front: Holly & ivy Christmas cake**

# SANTA'S STOCKING

*Preparation time: decorating the cake*
*Cooking time: about 1 hour 15–20 minutes*
*Oven: 160°C, 325°F, Gas Mark 3*

1 × 5-egg quantity Madeira Cake mixture (page 16)
1 recipe quantity Apricot Glaze (page 27)
1 recipe quantity Marzipan (page 22)
red and greed food colourings
narrow gold, green and/or red Christmas ribbons
chocolate money
½ recipe quantity vanilla Butter Cream (page 26)

This is another idea for a Christmas party cake, or for those who prefer a lighter Christmas cake but still favour marzipan. For a smaller stocking use a 28 × 18 × 4 cm/ 11 × 7 × 1½ inch tin and a 4-egg quantity of Madeira Cake mixture. Bake for about 50 minutes.

1. Spread out the cake mixture in a lined 30 × 25 × 5 cm/12 × 10 × 2 inch tin.
2. Bake in a preheated oven for about 1 hour 15–20 minutes or until well risen and firm to the touch. Turn on to a wire rack and leave to cool.
3. Draw a 'stocking' on a sheet of paper the same size as the cake, following the diagram. Cut out and place on the cake.
4. Cut around the stocking shape with a sharp knife and place the stocking-shaped cake on a cake board. Cut two or three parcels from the cake trimmings.
5. Brush all over the stocking and parcels with apricot glaze.
6. Take three-quarters of the marzipan and colour it red with food colouring. Roll out between two sheets of polythene and use to cover the stocking completely. Make a few holly berries from the marzipan trimmings.
7. Colour half the remaining marzipan green. Roll out and cut out six holly leaves (see page 52). Use the remaining green marzipan to cover the largest of the cake parcels.
8. Roll out the remaining uncoloured marzipan and use to cover the other cake parcels. Tie appropriate coloured ribbons round the parcels.
9. Position the parcels and chocolate money at the top of the stocking as if spilling out.
10. Put some of the butter cream into a piping bag fitted with a thick writing nozzle and pipe 'HAPPY CHRISTMAS' along the stocking.
11. Put the rest of the butter cream into a piping bag fitted with a star nozzle and pipe several rows of stars or shells at the top of the stocking to represent fur.
12. Attach the holly leaves and berries to the foot of the stocking with butter cream. Leave to set.

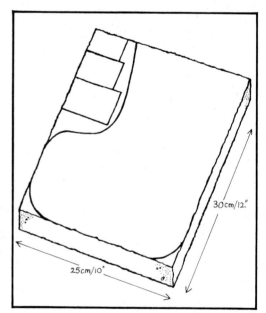

# CHRISTMAS TREE CAKE

*Preparation time: icing and decorating the cake*

1 × 20 cm/8 inch round Christmas Cake (page 74)
1 recipe quantity Apricot Glaze (page 27)
575 g/1¼ lb Marzipan (page 22)
Royal Icing made with 900 g/2 lb icing sugar (page 24)
red or yellow food colourings

DECORATION:
40 g/1½ oz Marzipan (page 22)
food colourings
56 silver balls

1. Brush the top and sides of the cake with apricot glaze, then cover with marzipan (see page 22). Leave to dry. Attach the cake to a silver cake board with a dab of icing.
2. Flat ice the cake all over (see pages 24 and 25), giving it two coats. Leave to dry completely.
3. To make the Christmas trees, colour all but a tiny piece of the marzipan a darkish green by kneading in green, blue and possibly a touch of brown food colourings. Roll out between two sheets of polythene or cling film and cut out eight Christmas trees about 5 cm/2 inches high (see page 52).
4. Colour the reserved piece of marzipan red using red paste food colouring and use to make eight 'tubs' for the trees. Attach and leave to dry.
5. Position a silver ball at each point. Leave to dry.
6. Colour a small amount of icing either red or yellow and put into a piping bag fitted with a medium writing nozzle. Half fill another piping bag fitted with a medium nozzle with white icing.
7. Make a curved template (see page 37), cut from an 18 cm/7 inch circle of paper. Position on the cake.
8. Outline the template with white icing, then remove the template and pipe a second line about 5 mm/¼ inch away from the first. Allow to dry, then overpipe in red or yellow icing.
9. Position four Christmas trees on top of the cake with the tubs opposite the inward point of the curve of the piping. Attach with a dab of icing.
10. Position the other trees around the side of the cake directly below the alternate point of the curves of icing; attach with icing.
11. Using a thick writing nozzle and white icing, pipe a large dot at the point of each curve of outline on the outside line of icing and two smaller dots in a straight line towards the edge of the cake. Complete with a final small dot using white icing and a medium nozzle.
12. Using the thick writing nozzle, pipe a border of large dots all round the top edge of the cake just overlapping on to the side edge.
13. Repeat with a heavy border of dots round the base of the cake.
14. Using the same nozzle, make a series of dots on the side of the cake equidistant from each Christmas tree, with a line of four dots of decreasing size in the centre and one of three dots on each side. Leave to dry.

# YULE LOG

*Preparation time: icing and decorating
the cake*
*Cooking time: 10–15 minutes*
*Oven: 200°C, 400°F, Gas Mark 6*

3 eggs
75 g/3 oz caster sugar
65 g/2½ oz self-raising flour
1 tablespoon cocoa powder
150 ml/¼ pint double or whipping
  cream, whipped, or vanilla or
  brandy Butter Cream (page 26)
1 recipe quantity ingredients for
  Chocolate Icing (page 19)

**DECORATION:**

little icing sugar
Marzipan Holly Leaves and
  Berries (page 52)
Marzipan Robin (page 76) or
  Christmas Roses (page 45)

1. Whisk the eggs and sugar together in a heatproof bowl over a pan of simmering water until very thick and the beater leaves a heavy trail when lifted. (If using an electric mixer, no heat is needed.) Remove from the heat and continue to beat until the mixture is cool.
2. Sift the flour and cocoa together twice, then fold lightly and evenly into the beaten mixture.
3. Pour into a greased and lined 30 × 23 cm/12 × 9 inch Swiss roll tin, spreading it right into the corners.
4. Bake in a preheated oven for 10–15 minutes or until just firm to the touch.
5. Turn out the cake on to a sheet of non-stick silicone paper or on to greaseproof paper sprinkled with caster sugar.
6. Trim the edges of the cake while still hot and immediately roll up with the paper inside. Allow to cool on a wire rack.
7. Carefully unroll cake and remove the paper. Spread all over with most of the whipped cream or butter cream. Re-roll carefully and place on a foil-covered oblong board or a plate.
8. If you want a branch on the log, cut a 5 cm/2 inch piece from the end of the cake at an angle and position it on one side of the cake.
9. Make up the chocolate icing with a little more icing sugar than specified. Leave until it begins to thicken, then spread all over the cake, including the ends.
10. Mark with a fork or palette knife along the length of the roll and the branch to resemble the 'bark' and leave to set.
11. Put the remaining cream or butter cream in a piping bag fitted with a thick writing nozzle and mark the filling on the ends. Leave to dry.
12. Sprinkle lightly with sifted icing sugar and decorate with holly leaves and berries and a robin or Christmas roses.

# RIBBON & HOLLY CAKE

*Preparation time: icing and decorating the cake*

1 × 18 cm/7 inch or 20 cm/8 inch square Christmas Cake (page 74)

1 recipe quantity Apricot Glaze (page 27)

700 g/1½ lb Marzipan (page 22)

Royal Icing made with 900 g/2 lb icing sugar (page 24)

**DECORATION:**

about 1 metre red ribbon, 4 cm/1½ inches wide

about 1 metre green ribbon, not more than 2 cm/¾ inch wide

silver balls

about 7 Marzipan Holly Leaves and Berries (page 52)

1. Brush the top and sides of the cake with apricot glaze, then cover with marzipan (see page 22). Leave to dry. Attach the cake to a silver cake board with a dab of icing.
2. Flat ice the cake all over (see pages 24 and 25), giving it two coats. Leave to dry.
3. Attach the centre of the red ribbon to the centre base of one side of the cake with two pins. Place the green ribbon in the centre of the red and secure with a dab of icing. Fold the ribbons up and over the top of the cake as in the picture and down the other side; attach with icing.
4. Using a piping bag fitted with a medium writing nozzle and white icing, pipe evenly spaced straight lines across the cake between the ribbons and almost up to them (leave space for a row of dots). Leave to dry.
5. Turn the cake round and complete the lattice by piping groups of four lines at right angles to the first with about 1 cm/½ inch between the groups, almost up to the ribbons. Leave to dry.
6. Using the same nozzle, pipe a row of small dots between the lattice and ribbon to give it an edging. Wrap the piping bag in polythene to use later.
7. Put some icing in a piping bag fitted with a thick writing nozzle and pipe a continuous looped edging round the top edge of the cake (except where the ribbon overlaps the edge).
8. Under each alternate loop pipe a large dot on the side of the cake with a smaller one under it. Complete with a third dot using the medium writing nozzle.
9. Pipe large dots with the larger nozzle around the base of the cake to seal it to the board. Put a silver ball in every second or third dot. Then pipe two smaller dots above alternate base border dots to match those on the top border.
10. Pipe a line of dots down each corner of the cake.
11. Complete the top decoration by adding bunches of two or three holly leaves and berries on the lattice each side of the ribbon. Leave to dry.

# NOVELTY CAKES

Novelty or fun cakes can be made for any occasion, particularly children's birthdays. All children love to have a surprise cake, preferably one that is completely different from anything they have seen before. It could be a tractor or a windmill cake and the ideas which follow feature many shapes which are imaginative, yet simple enough to tackle.

Birthdays aren't the only occasions when a novelty cake would be welcome. For instance, a party for Hallowe'en might call for a jack o'lantern cake. A silver or golden wedding party couple might prefer a sponge cake and a softer icing than the traditional royal icing. And a cake that looks like a basket full of flowers could suit anything from Mothers' Day to a retirement party.

The cakes suggested for use as a base are mainly Quick Mix, Madeira or Victoria Sponge (pages 12, 16 and 17). Any flavour can be used and the colours for icings and decorations can also be altered to your preferences. Rich or Economical Fruit Cakes (pages 10 and 75) can be used as an alternative provided they are baked in the tin specified in the recipe. (For piping techniques see pages 31–34.)

If difficulty is found in obtaining cake boards of correct size or shape for these cakes, it is quite simple to make your own by cutting several thicknesses of cardboard to the required size and then covering the built-up board with foil. Alternatively, use a wooden or other type of chopping board covered in foil.

# BIRTHDAY PARCEL

*Preparation time: about 20 minutes, plus icing and decorating*
*Cooking time: about 50 minutes*
*Oven: 160°C, 325°F, Gas Mark 3*

3-egg Quick Mix Cake mixture (page 12)

2 recipe quantities Chocolate Icing (page 19)

white or pastel satin ribbon, about 2.5 cm/1 inch wide

Marzipan Flowers and Leaves (pages 50 and 52)

1 recipe quantity Glacé Icing (page 20)

1. Bake the cake in a greased and floured 20 cm/8 inch square deep cake tin in a preheated oven for about 50 minutes or until well risen and firm to the touch. Turn on to a wire rack and leave to cool.
2. Place the cake on a 23 cm/9 inch square silver cake board.
3. Make up the chocolate icing using a little less icing sugar than stated to give a smoother icing.
4. Pour the icing over the cake and use a palette knife dipped in hot water to help cover the cake completely. Leave to set.
5. Carefully lay the ribbon over the cake to 'tie up the parcel'. A bow can be made for the centre, too.
6. Arrange a selection of marzipan flowers and leaves beside the ribbon, attaching with dabs of glacé icing.
7. Put the remaining glacé icing into a paper icing bag without a nozzle. Cut off just the tip and write the name or a message in one empty square below the ribbon. Leave to dry.

# FLOWER BASKET

*Preparation time: icing and decorating the cake*

1 × 20 cm/8 inch square Rich Fruit Cake (page 10), Madeira Cake (page 16) or Quick Mix Cake (page 12)

1 recipe quantity Apricot Glaze (page 27)

800 g/1¾ lb Marzipan (page 22)

Royal Icing, made with 900 g/2 lb icing sugar (page 24)

½ recipe quantity Gelatine or Moulding Icing (pages 20 and 21)

2 teaspoons glycerine

about 1 metre coloured ribbon to tone with flowers

30 cm/12 inch cane, or thick wire and silver foil for basket handle

fresh flowers and leaves and/or fern

The basket can be iced in any colour you wish instead of white. Butter Cream (page 26) can be used to ice a Madeira or quick mix cake, instead of royal icing. The marzipan can then either be used or omitted. If fresh flowers do not appeal, use Frosted or Crystallized Flowers (see page 40) or Marzipan or Moulding Icing Flowers (pages 50 and 51). As an alternative, use Frosted Fruits (page 40).

1. Brush the top and sides of the cake with apricot glaze, then cover with marzipan (see page 22). Leave to dry. Attach the cake to a cake board with a dab of icing.
2. Flat ice the cake with royal icing (see pages 24 and 25), giving one coat to the sides and two coats to the top. Leave to dry for 24 hours.
3. Tint the moulding icing to match the colour of the basket (if not to be white) and roll out to a square the same size as the top of the cake; the consistency of the icing should be fairly firm. Trim the square so it is a little smaller than the top of the cake, then cut it in half to give two triangles. Leave to dry for 24 hours in a warm place.
4. Add the extra glycerine to the remaining royal icing and use to fill two icing bags, one fitted with medium writing nozzle and the other with a basket weave nozzle.
5. Make a basket work design all round the sides of the cake (see page 34), then all over the two pieces of the lid. Leave to dry.
6. Pipe a thick line of icing across the centre of the cake from corner to corner and position the two lids so they are partly open – they will need to be supported with matchboxes or similar objects. Leave to dry.
7. Wind ribbons round the cane or several thicknesses of wire covered with foil. Bend for the handle. Attach the ends to the cake with icing and hold in place until set.
8. Tie a bow of ribbon and place in between the joins of the lids under the handle.
9. On the day the cake is to be served, arrange sprays of fresh flowers and leaves in the open ends of the basket. Tiny roses, fuchsias freesias, lilies of the valley, narcissi, etc, make an effective display.

# HALLOWE'EN CAKE

*Preparation time: 25–60 minutes*
*Cooking time: see method*
*Oven: 160°C, 325°F, Gas Mark 3*

3-egg orange Quick Mix Cake
   mixture (page 12) or Madeira
   Cake mixture (page 16)
225 g/8 oz Marzipan (page 22)
food colourings
1½ recipe quantities Butter Cream
   (page 26), or 1 recipe quantity
   American Frosting (page 19) or
   Seven Minute Frosting (page 19)

Alternatively, a Victoria Sponge Cake (page 17) mixture may be used. It should be baked at an oven temperature of 190°C, 375°F, Gas Mark 5 for about 40 minutes. If using a frosting to cover the cake, the decorations must all be made in advance. Otherwise the frosting will set before you have time to attach the decorations.

1. Bake the cake mixture in a greased and floured 23 cm/9 inch plain ring mould in a preheated oven. Allow 40–45 minutes for a quick mix cake or 1–1¼ hours for a Madeira cake. Cool on a wire rack.

2. To make the marzipan cats and witches, draw a paper pattern for the shapes and cut out. Colour about half the marzipan black (if you can't find black food colouring use a mixture of green, brown and blue) and roll out thinly. Cut out four witches on broomsticks and four cats by running a sharp knife all round the paper pattern. Leave to dry. Using butter cream a nose, eyes and whiskers can be piped on each cat. Facial features can be piped too, on the witches.

3. For the broomsticks, colour about 25 g/1 oz marzipan dark brown or black and leave 25 g/1 oz marzipan yellow. Roll the brown marzipan into eight broom handles. Mould the yellow marzipan into eight broom heads: first make a bell shape and cut it all over with a round-bladed knife for the bristles; add a bit more marzipan and repeat for more bristles. Attach the heads to the handles and leave to dry.

4. For the marzipan moons and stars, colour the remaining marzipan orange. Roll out and use cocktail cutters to make the shapes. Alternatively, cut them out freehand with the help of a sharp narrow-pointed knife.

5. Tint the butter cream or frosting orange with food colouring. If using butter cream, first mask the cake completely and smooth with a palette knife. If using frosting, simply swirl it thickly all over the cake and arrange the figures, cats and broomsticks evenly round the sides.

6. Mark the cake into eight sections. Place a marzipan witch in every alternate portion and a cat in the other spaces.

7. Put a broomstick between each witch and cat.

8. Attach the half moons and stars. Leave to dry.

# FLYING SAUCER

*Preparation time: icing and decorating the cake*

1 × 900 ml/1½ pint pudding basin Quick Mix Cake (page 12)
1 × 23 cm/9 inch round Quick Mix Cake (page 12)
1 recipe quantity Apricot Glaze (page 27)
450 g/1 lb Marzipan (page 22)
orange food colouring
1 recipe quantity Butter Cream (page 26)
orange-flavoured chocolate matchsticks
chocolate money
plastic spacemen figures (optional)

If the basin cake seems a bit too deep for the round cake, trim off a small portion to fit.

1. Place the round cake on a cake board and brush all over with apricot glaze.
2. Colour the marzipan orange with food colouring. Roll out two-thirds of the marzipan and use to cover the top and sides of the round cake.
3. Place the basin cake on top of the round cake, in the centre, with the rounded part up. Brush with apricot glaze.
4. Roll out the remaining marzipan and use to cover the basin cake, trimming the edges.
5. Colour the butter cream orange and put into a piping bag fitted with a five star nozzle.
6. Pipe a row of whirls round the base of the saucer and pipe a row of stars round the base of the basin.
7. Arrange a circle of chocolate matchsticks all round the outer part of the saucer, attaching with butter cream. Similarly, attach a circle of matchsticks to the top of the saucer.
8. Stick chocolate money in two rows round the cake with butter cream. Leave to set.
9. Plastic figures of spacemen may be placed around the saucer on the cake board.

# FLOWER CAKE

*Preparation time: icing and decorating
    the cake*

2 × 20 cm/8 inch Quick Mix Cakes
    (page 12) or Victoria Sponge
    Cakes (page 17) or a 3-egg
    Madeira Cake (page 16)
about 175 g/6 oz lemon curd or jam
1 recipe quantity Apricot Glaze
    (page 27)
100 g/4 oz walnuts or toasted
    almonds, chopped
225 g/8 oz Marzipan (page 22)
food colourings
few mimosa balls
artificial butterflies or bees

The petals of the flower can be of any
colour you choose, i.e. yellow with a pink
centre, white with a pink or yellow centre,
mauve, etc. Coarsely grated chocolate may
be used instead of nuts to cover the side of
the cake.

1.  Sandwich the cake layers together with
lemon curd or jam. If using a Madeira cake
cut it in half first.
2.  Brush all round the sides of the cake
with apricot glaze, then roll in walnuts or
almonds to give an even covering round
the sides and 5 cm/2 inches on to the top.
Place the cake on a cake board.
3.  Brush the top of the cake with apricot
glaze.
4.  Tint most of the marzipan pink (or any
other colour), kneading until evenly
coloured. Roll out thinly between two
sheets of polythene. Cut into eight petal
shapes about 10 cm/4 inches long and 5–
6 cm/2 inches at the widest part of the
petal.

5.  Curve the edges of the petals up a little
and flute the edges. Arrange on top of the
cake so they all touch in the centre and
also reach the edge of the cake.
6.  Form the remaining piece of yellow
marzipan into a centre for the flower and
stick it on with a little apricot glaze.
Mimosa balls can be stuck all over it to
represent the centre of a real daisy.
7.  Position butterflies or bees between the
petals and on the flower itself.

# GONE FISHING CAKE

*Preparation time: icing and decorating the cake*

2 × 20 cm/8 inch round Quick Mix Cakes (page 12)

175 g/6 oz jam

1 recipe quantity Apricot Glaze (page 27)

1 recipe quantity Gelatine or Moulding Icing (pages 20 and 21)

food colourings

½ recipe quantity Butter Cream (page 26)

165 g/5½ oz Marzipan (page 22)

9 Marzipan Flowers and 9 Leaves (pages 50 and 52)

1 Marzipan Boy (page 49)

1. Sandwich the cakes together with the jam and place on a 23 cm/9 inch round cake board.
2. Brush the cake all over with apricot glaze.
3. Tint the icing a pale blue by kneading in blue liquid food colouring until even. Roll out and use to cover the cake completely. Leave to dry.
4. Tint the butter cream green. Put into a piping bag fitted with a medium star nozzle and pipe touching stars all over about half the top of the cake to represent grass. Continue the stars all round the edge of the cake to form a border of 'grass'. Pipe another border of green stars all round the base of the cake.
5. Use about 120 g/4½ oz of the marzipan to make about 10 fishes of varying colours and shapes. Using a fine paint brush and food colouring, paint scales, eyes, etc., on the fish. Leave to dry.
6. To make the frog, colour all but 15 g/ ½ oz of the remaining marzipan green.

Break off about one-third and shape the remainder into a body. Make a cut into the thicker end of the body and shape the head slightly upwards. Halve the lower end of the body and shape into two front feet. Press the body of the frog so it has a big head and two bulging eyes. Use the reserved one-third of marzipan to make two back legs and feet. Attach to the body. Finally, paint on eyes, toes and dots all over the body with food colouring and a paint brush. Leave to dry.
7. Attach the fishes evenly round the sides of the cake using a dab of butter cream for each.
8. Place the marzipan boy on the top of the cake on a marzipan stool made from the last piece of marzipan. Place the frog in front of him and flowers and leaves beside him.
9. For the fishing rod attach a piece of fine string or thread to a cocktail stick and stick under the boy's arm.

# BUTTERFLY CAKE

*Preparation time: icing and decorating the cake*

2 × 20 cm/8 inch round chocolate Victoria Sponge Cakes (page 17)
1½–2 recipe quantities Butter Cream (page 26)
1 recipe quantity Apricot Glaze (page 27)
pink food colouring
coloured or silver balls
candles and holders

The Victoria sponge cake can be made any flavour you choose or a 3-egg Quick Mix Cake (page 12) can be halved and used as an alternative.

1. Use a little of the butter cream to sandwich the cakes together.
2. Cut the sandwich cake evenly in half. Position the halves back-to-back on a cake board at a slightly slanting angle so the 'wings' are wider apart at the top.
3. Brush the cake with apricot glaze.
4. Coat the cake all over with white (or coloured) butter cream. Then, with a serrated edge icing comb, pull all round the sides of the cake evenly.
5. Tint the remaining butter cream pink. Put into a piping bag fitted with a fine star nozzle and pipe a shell outline at the base of the wings to give two distinct shapes. Using a shell outline, pipe two shapes on the top of each wing.

6. Put the remaining icing into a piping bag fitted with a thick writing nozzle. Use to work a lacework design inside the shell shapes on the wings.
7. Work a line of shells all round the edge of the wings to form a border and add coloured or silver balls at intervals for decorations.
8. Pipe a 'body' between the two cakes using the same nozzle, building it up with two or three rows of butter cream in a backwards and forwards design.
9. Pipe a border of butter cream down each corner of the wings and all round the base of the butterfly. Leave to set.
10. Complete the cake with two candles in holders or strips of angelica for antennae. Position the rest of the candles in whirls of buttercream on the cake board.

# THE HOUSE AT POOH CORNER

*Preparation time: icing and decorating the cake*

1 × 30 × 25 × 5 cm/12 × 10 × 2 inch Quick Mix Cake (page 12)

1 recipe quantity Apricot Glaze (page 27)

1 recipe quantity Gelatine or Moulding Icing (see pages 20; 21)

green food colouring

1 tablespoons cocoa powder

Winnie the Pooh Characters (page 48)

1 recipe quantity Glacé Icing (page 20)

red or green satin ribbon

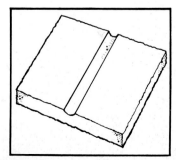

Any book title, song, nursery rhyme, etc, can be used with models or characters iced flat on to the pages. For example, for 'Mary, Mary, Quite Contrary', cover the cake in yellow icing and make marzipan flowers to represent bells and cockle shells and a model Mary holding a watering can (page 49).

A thin layer of marzipan can be added to the cake before the icing which will make the finished cake much smoother. Brush the marzipan with egg white before attaching the icing.

1. Place the cake on a cake board. Cut out a slightly rounded strip down the centre of the cake (see diagram).
2. Brush the cake all over with apricot glaze.
3. Tint the moulding or gelatine icing a pale green, then roll out most of it to a large rectangle to cover the whole of the cake and the sides. (If it is easier, roll out the icing in two pieces, one for each 'page' of the book.) Make cuts at the corners to shape evenly and press on to the edges of the cake to give square corners.

4. Tint the surplus icing brown by kneading in the sifted cocoa. Roll out and cut into narrow strips to place all round the base of the cake to represent the book's cover. Attach the strips to the cake with apricot glaze.
5. With a round-bladed knife, make cuts into the green icing on the sides of the 'book' to represent pages. Leave to set.
6. Position the Winnie the Pooh characters on the left hand page of the book, leaving space for the title.
7. Put the glacé icing into a piping bag fitted with a thick writing nozzle. Pipe the words 'THE HOUSE AT POOH CORNER' in between the characters on the cake, then attach the models with a dab of icing.
8. On the other page pipe the words from the beginning of the first chapter in the book using a medium writing nozzle and glacé icing: 'One day when Pooh Bear had nothing else to do, he thought he would do something, so he went round to Piglet's house . . .'
9. Position the ribbon down the centre of the pages in the cut out indentation as a book mark to complete the cake.

# LIGHTHOUSE CAKE

*Preparation time: decorating the cake*

1 × 29 × 21 × 4 cm/
11½ × 8½ × 1½ inch or
30 × 25 × 5 cm/12 × 10 × 2 inch
Quick Mix Cake (page 12)
1 recipe quantity Apricot Glaze
(page 27)
2 recipe quantities Butter Cream
(page 26)
pink, red or orange, yellow and
blue food colourings

Similar in shape, the lighthouse and windmill cakes can either lie flat on a board or stand upright. To make the lighthouse on this page stand upright, make the square cake and assemble it as in the windmill (see right).

1. Make a pattern as in the diagram and cut out. Position on the cake and cut out. Transfer the lighthouse to a large cake board. Cut the surplus cake into 'rocks' and place around the base of the cake on the board, attaching with apricot glaze.
2. Brush the cake all over with apricot glaze. Mark the lighthouse into four sections horizontally under the top piece left for the light.
3. Divide the butter cream into quarters. Leave one part white and use to spread over two of the sections on the lighthouse. Put the remaining white butter cream into a piping bag fitted with a scroll or rope nozzle and set aside.

4. Colour a second portion of the butter cream a deep pink, red or orange and use to fill in the other two portions on the lighthouse.
5. Colour another portion of butter cream yellow and spread some of it all over the top of the lighthouse for the light. With the white butter cream, pipe panes of glass over the yellow light.
6. Put the remaining yellow butter cream into a piping bag and with the scroll or rope nozzle pipe the lines of light radiating from the top of the lighthouse (omit this stage if making an upright lighthouse).
7. Pipe windows on the lighthouse with yellow butter cream and a yellow door at the base.
8. Tint the rest of the butter cream blue and put most of it into a piping bag fitted with a star nozzle. Use to pipe part way up the 'rocks', on the side of the lighthouse and on the board to represent the sea.
9. Using the scroll or rope nozzle, finish off the rocks with swirls of white butter cream to represent the breaking waves and spray.

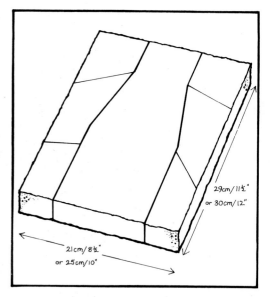

# WINDMILL CAKE

*Preparation time: icing and decorating the cake*

1 × 23 cm/9 inch square Quick Mix Cake (page 12) or Madeira Cake (page 16)

225 g/8 oz jam or lemon curd

1 recipe quantity Apricot Glaze (page 27)

2 recipe quantities Coffee Butter Cream (page 26)

food colourings

4 Chocolate Triangles about 10 cm/ 4 inches long (page 41)

100 g/4 oz Marzipan (page 22)

bought sugar flowers or Marzipan Flowers and Leaves (pages 50 and 52), in small sizes

Marzipan Boy and Girl (page 49)

Marzipan Dog (page 48)

1. Following the diagram cut the cake rounds, to give two 10 cm/4 inch rounds, two 7.5 cm/3 inch rounds and two 5 cm/ 2 inch rounds.
2. Assemble the rounds into a windmill shape on an 18 cm/7 inch square cake board. Begin with the largest rounds and stick all the rounds together with jam or lemon curd.
3. Brush the cake all over with apricot glaze.
4. Use coffee butter cream to mask the whole windmill, making it smooth and even-shaped.
5. Put the surplus butter cream into a piping bag fitted with a medium star nozzle. Pipe a shell decoration round the top of the windmill and a large rosette on the side of it towards the top. Attach the chocolate sails with another rosette of butter cream on top to secure.
6. Colour about 25 g/1 oz of the marzipan a deep colour to tone with the windmill.

Roll out the marzipan and cut out a door and three or four small windows. Position on the windmill.
7. Tint the remaining butter cream green and use to pipe flower stems up the sides of the windmill.
8. Tint the rest of the marzipan a grass green. Roll out thinly and use to cover the cake board, attaching with a little apricot glaze. Place the sugar or marzipan flowers at the top of the stems.
9. Position the marzipan characters on the grass, sticking them on with a little butter cream.

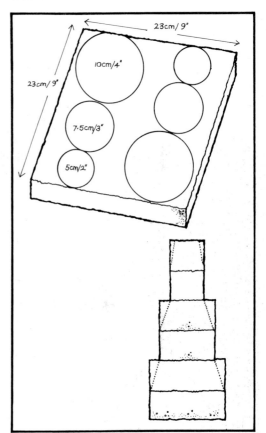

# PINK ELEPHANT CAKE

*Preparation time: icing and decorating the cake*

2 × 23 cm/9 inch round Quick Mix Cakes (page 12)

225 g/8 oz raspberry or apricot jam, or ½ recipe quantity flavoured Butter Cream (page 26)

1 recipe quantity Apricot Glaze (page 27)

2 recipe quantities Butter Cream (page 26)

pink food colouring

2 black sweets (for eyes)

candles and holders (optional)

If preferred, one deeper cake can be used without adding any filling.

1. Sandwich the cakes together with the jam or flavoured butter cream.
2. Draw a circle the same size as the cake on a piece of paper and draw a pattern for the head, ears and tusks, following the diagram. Cut out each piece and position on the cake. Mark round the pieces and then carefully cut out with a sharp knife.
3. Assemble the cake in the shape of an elephant on a cake board or piece of thick cardboard covered with foil. Stick the pieces of cake together with a little jam or flavoured butter cream.
4. Brush the cake all over with apricot glaze. Cover the tusks with butter cream using a round-bladed knife. Alternatively put butter cream into a piping bag fitted with a medium star nozzle and pipe lines, stars or shells to cover the tusks.
5. Reserve 1 tablespoon of butter cream for the eyes. Tint the remaining butter cream a pale to medium pink. Spread or pipe all over the elephant to cover it completely.

6. Pipe or spread a dot of white butter cream for each eye on the pink butter cream and add a black sweet for the pupil.
7. Candle holders and candles may be placed down the ears, and a name or 'HAPPY BIRTHDAY' can be piped under the eyes using a deeper coloured butter cream and a medium or thick writing nozzle. Leave to set. Desiccated coconut can be sprinkled on the remaining area of cake board.

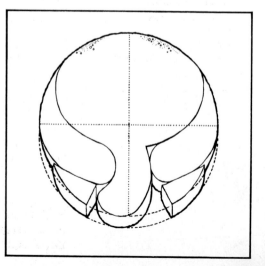

# THERE WAS AN OLD WOMAN WHO LIVED IN A SHOE

*Preparation time: about 20 minutes,
    plus icing and decorating*
*Cooking time: about 1 hour*
*Oven: 160°C, 325°F, Gas Mark 3*

2 × 3-egg Quick Mix Cake
    mixtures (page 12)
50 g/2 oz cornflour
2 recipe quantities Apricot Glaze
    (page 27)
1½ recipe quantities Butter Cream
    (page 26)
yellow food colouring
1–2 tablespoons sifted cocoa
    powder
chocolate buttons
coloured silver or mimosa balls
candles and holders
few Marzipan Flowers and Leaves
    (pages 50 and 52)

If preferred, the horizontal part of this cake can be split and filled with Butter Cream (page 26) or jam. For a special effect, the cake can be placed on a bed of desiccated coconut tinted green (see page 40), to represent grass.

1. Make the cake mixture, sifting the cornflour with the flour. Divide between two greased and floured 900 g/2 lb loaf tins. Bake in a preheated oven for about 1 hour or until well risen and firm to the touch. Turn on to a wire rack to cool.
2. Place the cakes on a cake board, trimming one end of one cake to form the roof as shown in the diagram. Stick the ends of the cakes together with butter cream or jam. Make the end of the other cake rounded for the toe.
3. Brush the cake all over with apricot glaze.
4. Tint most of the butter cream yellow and use to mask the whole cake. A 'brickwork' design can be marked all over using a round bladed knife. Pipe a star edging to the shoe.
5. Add sufficient cocoa to the remaining butter cream to tint it a dark brown. Put into a piping bag fitted with a thick writing nozzle.

6. Pipe windows on the 'shoe' and pipe a door on the side with a backwards and forwards action so each line touches the next.
7. 'Tile' the roof with chocolate buttons.
8. Mark the age of the child on the door using silver or mimosa balls and position the same number of candles in holders down the length of the foot. Laces can be piped between the candles using the brown butter cream.
9. Arrange marzipan flowers and leaves round the base of the shoe for a 'garden'.

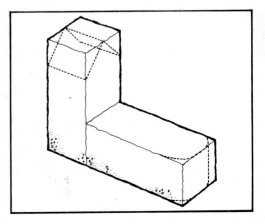

# YACHT CAKE

*Preparation time: icing and decorating the cake*

1 × 30 × 25 × 5 cm/12 × 10 × 2 inch Madeira Cake (page 16)

1 recipe quantity Apricot Glaze (page 27)

1½ recipe quantities Gelatine or Moulding Icing (pages 20 and 21)

food colourings

1 candy stick or stick of rock

½ recipe quantity Butter Cream (page 26)

1. Draw a paper pattern following the diagram and cut out. Position on the cake and carefully cut out the pieces, discarding surplus cake.
2. Brush each piece with apricot glaze.

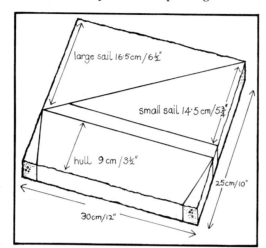

3. Roll out about one-third of the icing thinly and use to cover one of the 'sails'.
4. Roll out a second third and use to cover the second sail.
5. Tint the remaining icing a deep pink, red or green, kneading until the colour is even. Use to cover the hull.
6. Assemble the pieces of cake as in the picture on a cake board, using the candy stick for a mast. The sails should just touch the candy stick and boat. A paper flag can also be stuck on to the top of the mast.
7. Tint the butter cream a contrasting colour to the boat, making it fairly bright. Put into a piping bag fitted with a fine star nozzle and pipe a number on the sail and 'TODAY' beneath it. The name of the child can be piped on the boat itself.
8. A row of butter cream stars can be piped all round the base of the cake as a border in any colour but preferably blue to represent the sea. Leave to dry.

# ROUNDABOUT CAKE

*Preparation time: decorating and icing the cake*

2 or 3 × 23 cm/9 inch round Quick Mix Cakes (page 12)

100–225 g/4–8 oz lemon curd or raspberry jam

1½ recipe quantities Butter Cream (page 26)

30 cm/12 inch stick

aluminium foil

about 8 different coloured narrow ribbons each about ½ metre long

2 × 30 cm/12 inch circles of stiff paper or card in two colours

glue

about 2 packets chocolate fingers

food colourings

75 g/3 oz desiccated coconut

7 or 8 Marzipan Animals (pages 47 and 48); Frog (page 87); and Robin (page 76)

coloured silver balls

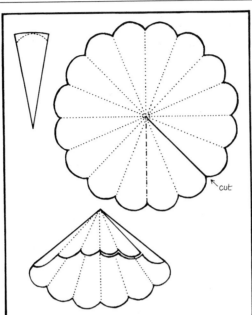

Chocolate animal biscuits can be used instead of marzipan animals, and a plain piece of coloured paper will make an alternative canopy.

1.  Sandwich the two or three cakes together, first adding a layer of lemon curd or jam and then a layer of butter cream.

2.  Place the cake on a cake board about 5 cm/2 inches larger than the cake.

3.  Cover the stick with foil, then wind two of the coloured ribbons round it. Push the stick right through the centre of the cake to the board.

4.  To make a roof for the roundabout fold one of the circles of paper or card into quarters then into eighths and then once more into sixteenths. Cut a scalloped edge as shown in the diagram. Open the circle which will have marked portions on it. From the second circle cut out seven scallop sections and glue these on to alternate areas of the canopy. Make a cut to the centre of the circle and fold two portions from one side over the first two on the other side (see diagram); attach with staples. Attach this to the top of the pole with a drawing pin. Use a small circle of paper or card to cover the drawing pin.

5.  Mask the whole cake with butter cream, reserving enough for decoration.

6.  Arrange chocolate finger biscuits all round the sides of the cake, cutting to length if necessary so the tips just show above the cake.

7.  Tint a bowl of warm water yellow with food colouring and stir in the coconut. Leave until the coconut takes up the colour, then drain very thoroughly with the help of a potato masher. Spread out on kitchen paper and leave in a warm place until completely dry. Spoon the yellow coconut evenly over the top of the cake.

8.  Arrange marzipan animals round the top of the cake. Attach the ribbons to the roof of the roundabout with staples.

9.  Colour the remaining butter cream orange or green. Put into a piping bag fitted with a fine or medium star nozzle and pipe large stars all round the base. Top each alternate star with a silver ball.

10.  Another row of stars with silver balls can also be piped on the top of the cake a little away from the central pole.

# HICKORY DICKORY DOCK CAKE

*Preparation time: icing and decorating the cake*

1 × 29 × 21 × 4 cm/
  11½ × 8½ × 1½ inch Quick Mix
  Cake (page 12)
coffee Glacé Icing, made with
  450 g/1 lb icing sugar (page 20)
100 g/4 oz Marzipan (page 22)
1 recipe quantity Butter Cream
  (page 26)
1–2 tablespoons sifted cocoa
  powder
15 chocolate buttons
1 Marzipan Mouse (page 47)

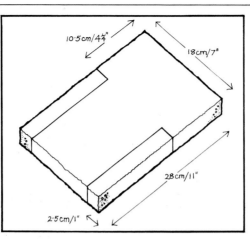

This cake is iced in shades of brown, but the colourings can be any you like.

1. Draw a paper pattern following the diagram. Cut out and place on the cake. Cut round the pattern with a sharp knife. Place on a cake board.
2. Coat the cake all over with glacé icing, using a palette knife dipped in hot water. Leave to dry, then cut off and remove any surplus icing around the base.
3. Roll out the marzipan and cut into two pieces, one 16.5 × 9 cm/6½ × 3½ inch rectangle (to fit the face of the clock) and the other a 6 × 5 cm/2½ × 2 inch rectangle for the 'works' of the clock. Position on the cake as shown.
4. Put a little butter cream in an icing bag fitted with a medium writing nozzle and pipe a wavy line all round the clock face and another decoration down the sides of the pendulum case.
5. Tint the rest of the butter cream a dark brown with cocoa and put some in a piping bag fitted with a fine or medium star nozzle. Pipe a shell edging round the top of the cake to outline the clock and round the base, making pointed corners. Pipe a line of shells down each side of the pendulum case.
6. Attach 15 chocolate buttons in the appropriate places round the clock face with butter cream. Using the white butter cream, pipe the numbers 1 to 12 evenly round the clock face.
7. Pipe clock hands to 1 o'clock with white butter cream. If the cake is for a birthday, the hands can point to the hour that corresponds with the age of the child.
8. Attach two chocolate buttons to the lower piece of marzipan. Pipe two lines of white butter cream for the pendulum chains on the marzipan.
9. With brown or white butter cream and the writing nozzle, write the beginning of the nursery rhyme: 'Hickory dickory dock the mouse ran up the clock' in the space below the pendulum.
10. Finally, position the marzipan mouse climbing up the clock.

# IGLOO CHRISTMAS CAKE

*Preparation time: icing and decorating*
*the cake*
*Cooking time: about 50 minutes*
*Oven: 160°C, 325°F, Gas Mark 3*

2-egg Quick Mix Cake mixture
  (page 12)
25 g/1 oz cornflour
1 recipe quantity Gelatine Icing or
  Moulding Icing (pages 20 and
  21)
food colourings
½ recipe quantity Chocolate
  Butter Cream (page 26)
1 recipe quantity Apricot Glaze
  (page 27)
1 mini chocolate-covered Swiss
  roll
50 g/2 oz plain chocolate
  desiccated coconut (optional)

This cake can be made in any flavour you like. It makes a good alternative to a rich fruit Christmas cake, and is ideal for a children's Christmas party. Gelatine or moulding icing can also be used to make nine holly leaves and tiny berries. Paint the leaves a dark green and the berries red; leave to dry.

1. Make up the cake mixture with the cornflour added and turn into a greased and floured 900 ml/1½ pint ovenproof pudding basin.
2. Bake in a preheated oven for about 50 minutes or until well risen and firm to the touch. Turn out on to a wire rack and cool.
3. Use 40 g/1½ oz of the gelatine or moulding icing to make the eskimo; keep the remainder in a polythene bag. Mould a round ball for the head and add a sausage shape all round for the fur on his hood. Shape a triangular piece for his body with arms crossed and attach the head. Lastly, make a block for his lower body and legs, standing it on a plinth; attach to the rest of the eskimo. Using a paint brush and blue or turquoise food colouring, paint the eskimo's coat and trousers. Change to brown colouring and paint his boots and

face. Mark eyes, nose and mouth with brown food colouring. Leave to dry.
4. Remove another 25 g/1 oz of the moulding icing and use to shape a husky dog (see page 48). Leave to dry.
5. Split the cake into two layers and sandwich together with the butter cream.
6. Place the cake on a large cake board and brush all over with the apricot glaze. Position the chocolate roll at one side of the cake for the entrance.
7. Roll out the remaining gelatine or moulding icing and take a small piece to cover the chocolate roll. Cut the rest of the icing to a 23 cm/9 inch round and lay over the cake. Carefully mould it to cover evenly and touch the board all round. Leave to dry.
8. Melt the chocolate in a heatproof bowl over a pan of hot water and put into a paper icing bag (page 29). Leave to cool and thicken a little, then cut just the tip off the bag. Use to mark the 'brickwork' all over the igloo.
9. Stand the eskimo and his dog outside the igloo and attach to the cake board with a little chocolate. Desiccated coconut can be used to cover the remaining area of cake board.

# TRACTOR CAKE

*Preparation time: icing and decorating the cake*

2 × 29 × 21 × 4 cm/
  11½ × 8½ × 1½ inch Quick Mix
  Cakes (page 12)

225 g/8 oz jam or lemon curd, or
  ½ recipe quantity Butter Cream
  (page 26)

1 recipe quantity Apricot Glaze
  (page 27)

2 recipe quantities Butter Cream
  (page 26)

yellow and brown food colourings

2 chocolate matchsticks or
  chocolate finger biscuits

1. Trim the cakes so they are even and have straight sides.
2. Draw a pattern for the tractor and two wheels on paper. Position on one of the cakes and cut out; repeat with the second cake to give two tractor 'bodies' and four wheels.
3. Sandwich the tractors together with jam, lemon curd or butter cream. Add a dab or two of butter cream to the cake base and stand up on a cake board. If necessary, keep in place with supports while the cakes set.
4. Position the wheels, two large at the back and two small at the front, on the sides of the tractor and attach with jam, lemon curd or butter cream.
5. Brush the cake with apricot glaze.

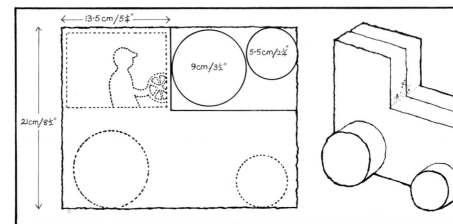

6. Colour about three-quarters of the butter cream yellow and spread all over the tractor except for the wheels.
7. Colour the rest of the butter cream brown and use to cover the wheels. Mark the tyre tread with a fork.
8. Put the remaining yellow butter cream into a piping bag fitted with a medium writing nozzle and use to pipe spokes and a wavy edging on the wheels.
9. Put the remaining brown butter cream into a piping bag fitted with a medium writing nozzle and pipe lines round the driver's cab. Pipe a steering wheel on each side of the cab and also one on the front of the cab.
10. Outline and pipe lines for the bonnet engine covers on each side and then pipe a rectangle on the front for the radiator, filling it in completely with brown butter cream.
11. Stick one or two chocolate matchsticks or finger biscuits on the bonnet for the exhaust system.
12. With the brown butter cream, outline and fill in the shape of a driver sitting in the cab, so you can see him from all sides.
13. If candles are required, position them down the length of the bonnet.

# STABLES CAKE

*Preparation time: about 30 minutes, plus icing and decorating*
*Cooking time: 45–50 minutes*
*Oven 160°C, 325°F, Gas Mark 3*

2-egg Quick Mix Cake mixture (page 12)

1 tablespoon cornflour

1 × 29 × 21 × 4 cm/ 11½ × 8½ × 1½ inch coffee Quick Mix Cake (page 12)

1½ recipe quantities coffee Butter Cream (page 26)

little chocolate vermicelli

about 25 g/1 oz chocolate dots

1–1½ packets chocolate finger biscuits

1–2 tablespoons sifted cocoa powder

about 100 g/4 oz Marzipan (page 22)

green, red and brown food colourings

100 g/4 oz digestive biscuits, crumbled

candles and holders (optional)

The flavours of the cakes can be altered to your preference.

1. Make up the 2-egg cake mixture, sifting the cornflour with the flour. Bake in a greased and floured 900 g/2 lb loaf tin in a preheated oven for 45–50 minutes or until well risen and firm to the touch. Cool on a wire rack.

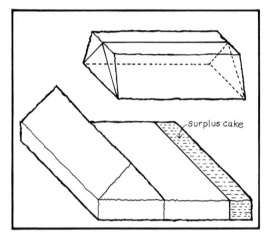

surplus cake

2. Cut the loaf cake to represent a roof, as shown in the diagram. Cut the slab cake into two equal pieces the same width as the base of the loaf cake – there will be a little surplus cake (see diagram).
3. Sandwich the two pieces of slab cake together with butter cream and put on the 'roof'. Place the cake on a 30 cm/12 inch round silver cake board.
4. Mask the whole cake in coffee butter cream, then cover the roof evenly with chocolate vermicelli, taking care not to let it spill over the 'walls'.
5. Put a line of chocolate dots all round the edge of the roof.
6. Cut chocolate finger biscuits in half and stick all round the base of the stable, leaving the front clear.
7. Beat sufficient cocoa into the remaining butter cream to turn it a dark brown. Put into a piping bag fitted with a medium writing nozzle.
8. Pipe a window high up on each end of the stable, adding shutters which can be filled in with up and down lines of butter cream using the same nozzle.
9. Outline the stable doors with the butter cream, then fill in the open upper doors and closed lower doors. Work a bolt on the lower doors and a strut of wood across the doors both top and bottom. Pipe a hitching ring to the right of each door on the wall and a pitch-fork and shovel leaning up against the wall.
10. When the butter cream walls are beginning to dry, mark 'brickwork' all over using a sharp knife.
11. Pipe brown butter cream in front of the stables to represent the flower beds.
12. Remove one-third of the marzipan and tint it red. Use to make 12–14 tiny flowers.
13. Roll out the remaining marzipan and cut into two strips the same width as the stable doors. Using the piping nozzle, write the names of two ponies on the strips and stick them over the doors.
14. Tint the remaining marzipan grass green and roll out thinly. Use a little to make leaves. Use the rest to cover the cake board, leaving the area in front of the doors bare. Sprinkle with the crushed biscuits for the stable yard.
15. Place the flowers and the leaves in the flower beds.
16. The required number of candles in holders can be stuck along the top of the roof.

# NUMERAL BIRTHDAY CAKES

*Preparation time; icing and decorating the cakes*

Quick Mix Cakes (page 12) or Madeira Cakes (page 16)

225 g/8 oz jam or ¼ recipe quantity Butter Cream, if necessary for sandwiching cakes together

1¾–2 recipe quantities Butter Cream (page 26)

food colouring and flavouring (optional)

candles and candle holders (optional)

jelly sweets (optional)

Marzipan Flowers (page 50)

Marzipan Leaves (page 52)

These cakes are especially fun for children and can be decorated in many ways to incorporate a hobby or child's special fancy. For a formally iced cake using marzipan and royal icing, a Rich Fruit Cake (page 10) can be used. Numerals cakes are fun for jubilee celebrations, length of service parties, retirements, etc. They make good anniversary cakes, especially for 25, 40 and 50 years. For a 40th or ruby wedding cake, decorate with chocolate butter cream, glacé cherries and grated chocolate or chocolate curls.

1. If using pairs of cakes sandwich them together with the jam or butter cream. Place on a cake board.

2. Tint the butter cream and add flavouring, if using. Use to mask the whole cake, perhaps finishing with a swirling design all over or backwards and forwards lines made with a round-bladed knife.

3. Tint the remaining butter cream a darker shade and put into a piping bag fitted with a star nozzle. Use to pipe a shell or star edging round the top edge and base of the cake.

4. Stick candles at intervals on the top of the cake. Alternatively, put seedless or sieved jam into a paper icing bag (see page 29), without a nozzle, then cut off the tip. Pipe a message on the top of the cakes.

5. Stick jelly sweets in a line round the sides, or pipe stars of butter cream.

6. Finally, position the marzipan flowers and leaves on top of the cakes, attaching with butter cream. Leave to set.

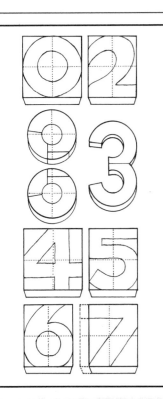

## SHAPING NUMERAL CAKES

**NOUGHT:** bake a 23–30 cm/9–12 inch round cake. When cold cut a 7.5–12.5 cm/ 3–5 inch diameter hole in centre.

**ONE:** bake a 15 cm/6 inch square sandwich cake. Cut in half and position one piece above the other.

**TWO:** bake a 29 × 21 × 4 cm/ 11½ × 8½ × 1½ inch slab cake or a 30 × 25 × 5 cm/12 × 10 × 2 inch cake. Cut a pattern, transfer to the cake and cut out.

**THREE:** bake 2 × 20 cm/8 inch round sandwich cakes. Cut out a pattern, transfer to the cakes and cut out. Stick the two cakes together with jam or butter cream.

**FOUR:** bake an 18–25 cm/7–10 inch square sandwich cake. Cut out a pattern, transfer to the cake and cut out, taking care when removing the middle piece.

**FIVE:** bake a 29 × 21 × 4 cm/ 11½ × 8½ × 1½ inch slab cake or a 30 × 25 × 5 cm/12 × 10 × 2 inch cake. Cut a pattern, transfer to the cake and cut out.

**SIX or NINE:** bake a 29 × 21 × 4 cm/ 11½ × 8½ × 1½ inch slab cake or a 30 × 25 × 5 cm/12 × 10 × 2 inch cake. Cut a pattern, transfer to the cake and cut out.

**SEVEN:** bake an 18–25 cm/7–10 inch square cake, or bake a 29 × 21 × 4 cm/ 11½ × 8½ × 1½ inch or a 30 × 25 × 5 cm/ 12 × 10 × 2 inch slab cake. Cut out a pattern, position on the cake and cut out.

**EIGHT:** bake 2 × 20 cm/8 inch round sandwich cakes. Cut out a pattern with a 7.5–9 cm/3–3½ inch circle out of the centre. Transfer to the cakes and cut out. Trim a piece off the side of each cake and sandwich together with jam or butter cream to make an eight.

# GATEAUX

Although the French word *gâteau* really only means a cake, the English have narrowed the meaning to cover those special cakes that are suitable to grace a party table, be it coffee time, tea time or an elegant dinner party. The base of the gâteau is usually a light-textured sponge, but meringue, shortbread or a combination of these and others are also often used. Choux paste may be added to give another dimension of texture. The fillings and decorations turn the basic cake into a masterpiece – and it is all so much easier to create than you might imagine.

Most of the basic cakes in this section can be made in advance and frozen, but it is best to assemble the gâteau just before it is required. Meringues can be made in advance, too, and stored in an airtight container. Choux paste can be baked and frozen, but is best refreshed in a moderate oven for a few minutes after thawing.

**Below left: Chocolate marron gâteau**
**Right: Black Forest chocolate roll**

# BLACK FOREST CHOCOLATE ROLL

*Serves 8*
*Preparation time: 30 minutes,*
*plus standing*
*Cooking time: about 20 minutes*
*Oven: 200°C, 400°F, Gas Mark 6*

3-egg chocolate Whisked Sponge Cake mixture (page 14)

FILLING AND DECORATION:

1 × 425 g/15 oz can black cherries

2 teaspoons arrowroot

300 ml/½ pint double or whipping cream

2–3 tablespoons Kirsch, brandy or cherry brandy

icing sugar

25–50 g/1–2 oz Chocolate Curls (page 40) (optional)

1. Bake the cake mixture in a greased and lined 30 × 23 cm/12 × 9 inch Swiss roll tin in a preheated oven for 12–15 minutes or until just firm to the touch.
2. Turn the cake immediately on to a sugar-dredged sheet of greaseproof paper placed on a damp tea towel. Peel off the lining paper and trim the cake edges. Carefully roll up the cake, with the paper inside. Leave to cool.
3. Meanwhile, prepare the filling. Drain the cherries, reserving 150 ml/¼ pint of the syrup (add water to make up to this quantity, if necessary). Put the syrup into a saucepan, stir in the arrowroot and bring to the boil, stirring. Simmer until thick and clear. Remove from the heat.
4. Reserve eight whole cherries or if the cherries are very large reserve four. Halve and stone the remainder and stir into the thickened syrup. Leave until quite cold.
5. Whip the cream until stiff. Put about one-third into a piping bag fitted with a star nozzle.
6. Unroll the cake carefully and remove the paper. Sprinkle the cake with the liqueur. Spread first with the cream and then with the cherry mixture. Carefully roll the cake again and place it on a serving plate.
7. Lightly dredge the cake with sifted icing sugar. Pipe the remaining cream along the centre top, making layers of stars or shells. Arrange chocolate curls, if used, along the top and finish with whole or halved and stoned black cherries on the cream. Leave for at least 1 hour for the flavours to marry before serving.

# CHOCOLATE MARRON GATEAU

*Serves 8*
*Preparation time: about 30 minutes,*
*plus standing*
*Cooking time: about 30 minutes*
*Oven: 190°C, 375°F, Gas Mark 5*

3 eggs (sizes 1, 2)

115 g/4½ oz caster sugar

75 g/3 oz plain flour

20 g/¾ oz cocoa powder

FILLING AND DECORATION:

1 × 425 g/15 oz can unsweetened chestnut purée

2 tablespoons clear honey

300 ml/½ pint double or whipping cream

grated rind of ½ lemon (optional)

3–4 tablespoons Grand Marnier, Cointreau or rum

100 g/4 oz block plain chocolate

4 marrons glacé or glacé fruits, halved

16 Chocolate Leaves (page 41)

1. Whisk the eggs and sugar together in a heatproof bowl over a pan of hot water until very pale and thick and the whisk leaves a heavy trail. (If using an electric beater, no heat is needed.) Remove from the heat.
2. Sift the flour and cocoa together twice, then fold quickly and evenly through the whisked mixture.
3. Turn into a greased and lined 28 × 18 × 4 cm/11 × 7 × 1½ inch tin. Bake in a preheated oven for about 30 minutes or until well risen and firm to the touch. Turn on to a wire rack to cool. Peel off the paper when cold.
4. Put the chestnut purée into a bowl and beat until very smooth, then beat in the honey. Put about one-quarter of the chestnut mixture into a piping bag fitted with a star vegetable nozzle.
5. Whip the cream until stiff and fold one-quarter of it into the remaining chestnut mixture with the lemon rind, if used.
6. Cut the cake in half lengthways. Sprinkle each half with liqueur and sandwich together with the chestnut cream.
7. Use the remainder of the whipped cream to mask the cake completely.
8. Using a potato peeler, pare the chocolate into small curls (see page 40). Use to coat the sides of the gâteau.
9. Pipe a row of stars or a shell design of chestnut purée along the centre top of the gâteau and decorate each side with 'flowers' made of half a marron glacé or glacé fruit and two or three chocolate leaves. Leave to stand for at least 1 hour before serving.

# COFFEE WALNUT CRUNCH GATEAU

*Serves 8–10*
*Preparation time: about 45 minutes,*
*plus chilling*
*Cooking time: 45–50 minutes*
*Oven: 190°C, 375°F, Gas Mark 5*

175 g/6 oz digestive biscuits,
crushed
50 g/2 oz walnuts, chopped
100 g/4 oz unsalted butter, melted

**COFFEE LAYER:**
150 g/6 oz butter or margarine
150 g/6 oz light soft brown sugar,
sifted
3 eggs (sizes 1, 2)
150 g/6 oz self-raising flour, sifted
1½ tablespoons coffee essence or
strong black coffee

**FILLING AND DECORATION:**
1 tablespoon coffee essence or
strong black coffee
1 recipe quantity Confectioner's
Custard (page 27)
100 g/4 oz apricot jam
1 recipe quantity coffee Butter
Cream (page 26)
50 g/2 oz walnuts, finely chopped
icing sugar
few walnut halves, to decorate

1. Mix together the biscuit crumbs and chopped walnuts and stir in the melted butter. Press over the bottom of a well-greased 20 cm/8 inch flan ring placed on a board or plate. Chill until required.
2. For the coffee layer, cream the butter or margarine and sugar together until light and fluffy. Beat in the eggs, one at a time, following each with 1 tablespoon of the flour. Fold in the remaining flour followed by the coffee essence or coffee.
3. Turn the mixture into a greased and base lined 20 cm/8 inch round deep cake tin and level the top.
4. Bake in a preheated oven for 45–50 minutes or until well risen and just firm to the touch. Turn on to a wire rack and leave to cool.
5. For the filling, stir the coffee essence or coffee into the confectioner's custard. Cover with cling film and, if necessary, leave to cool.
6. To assemble the gâteau, remove the flan ring from the biscuit base and spread the apricot jam over it. Cut the cake into two layers and position one layer over the jam. Cover with the coffee custard and place the second cake layer on top.

7. Put half the coffee butter cream into a piping bag fitted with a star nozzle. Spread the sides of the gâteau with the remaining butter cream and coat with the chopped walnuts. Dredge the top of the gâteau heavily with sifted icing sugar, then pipe a wheel design and outside border on top of the cake with butter cream. Make a whirl in each section and top each with a walnut half.

**VARIATION:**
The cake may be sprinkled with 4 tablespoons Tia Maria or other coffee liqueur before assembling.

# GINGERED GATEAU

*Serves 8*
*Preparation time: about 40 minutes*
*Cooking time: about 25 minutes*
*Oven: 160°C, 325°F, Gas Mark 3*

125 g/5 oz butter or margarine
100 g/4 oz light soft brown sugar,
sifted
150 g/6 oz plain flour
1 teaspoon bicarbonate of soda
2 teaspoons ground ginger
2 eggs (sizes 1, 2)
1 tablespoon black treacle
1 tablespoon golden syrup
1 tablespoon milk

**FILLING AND DECORATION:**
3 tablespoons brandy
1 recipe quantity Confectioner's
Custard (page 27)
150 ml/¼ pint double or whipping
cream
2 tablespoons milk
1 tablespoon sifted icing sugar
8 Brandy Cornets, made from half
recipe quantity (page 122)
few pieces of stem ginger

This cake is best made and filled with confectioner's custard the day before required. Add the cream and brandy cornets just before serving. The brandy cornets may be made several days in advance and stored in an airtight container.

1. Cream the butter or margarine and sugar together until very light and fluffy.
2. Sift the flour, bicarbonate of soda and ginger together. Beat the eggs into the creamed mixture, one at a time, following each with a spoonful of the flour mixture. Fold in the remaining flour followed by the treacle, syrup and milk.
3. Spread the mixture evenly in a greased and lined 30 × 23 cm/12 × 9 inch Swiss roll tin, making sure there is plenty in the corners.
4. Bake in a preheated oven for about 25 minutes or until set and just firm. Cool on a wire rack.
5. Beat 2 tablespoons of the brandy into the confectioner's custard. Cover with cling film and, if necessary, leave to cool.

6. Whip the cream and milk together until stiff, then mix in the icing sugar and remaining brandy.
7. Cut the cake into three equal rectangles and sandwich together with the brandy custard. Place on a serving plate and spread the top of the gâteau with some of the brandy cream.
8. Pipe a whirl of cream into each of the brandy cornets and top each with a piece of stem ginger. Arrange the cornets, head to tail, along the top of the gâteau.

# LEMON GATEAU

Serves 8
Preparation time: about 40 minutes
Cooking time: about 25 minutes

1 round lemon Torten Sponge
  Cake (page 15)
225 g/8 oz lemon curd
450 ml/¾ pint double or whipping
  cream
50 g/2 oz flaked almonds, toasted

GLAZED LEMON SLICES:
8 lemon slices (5 mm/¼ inch
  thick), whole or halved
75 g/3 oz caster sugar

1. First make the glazed lemon slices.
Remove any pips from the lemon slices
and place in a frying pan. Cover with
water, then poach gently for about 20
minutes or until tender, adding more
water if necessary.
2. Drain the lemon slices and place on a
baking sheet.
3. Add the sugar to the water left in the
pan and stir to dissolve. Bring to the boil
and boil to reduce to a thick glaze.
4. Pour the glaze over the lemon slices
and leave to cool.
5. Cut the cooled cake into three equal
layers. Place the base layer on a serving
plate and spread with half the lemon curd.
6. Whip the cream until stiff and spread a
thin layer over the lemon curd. Cover with
the second cake layer. Spread over the
remaining lemon curd and a little cream,
then top with the final cake layer.

7. Use most of the remaining cream to
mask the cake completely. Put the rest of
the cream into a piping bag fitted with a
medium star nozzle.
8. Press the toasted almonds on to the
sides of the gâteau, using a round-bladed
knife or palette knife for ease.
9. Arrange the glazed lemon slices in an
overlapping circle on top of the gâteau.
Complete with a shell edging of piped
cream around the top edge. A similar
edging can also be added around the base.

### VARIATION:
For an orange gâteau, replace the lemon
rind in the torten sponge cake with orange
rind; the lemon curd with orange curd or
orange marmalade; and glazed lemon
slices with halved glazed orange slices
from a small thin-skinned orange.

# STRAWBERRY GATEAU

*Serves 8*
*Preparation time: about 30 minutes*

300 ml/½ pint double or whipping cream
1 recipe quantity Confectioner's Custard (page 27)
350 g/12 oz strawberries
1 round vanilla Torten Sponge Cake (page 15)
few Chocolate Triangles (page 41)

1. Whip the cream until thick. Fold about half of it carefully into the confectioner's custard.
2. Reserve eight whole strawberries for decoration and slice the remainder lengthways.
3. Cut the cake into three equal layers. Place the base layer on a serving plate and spread with two-thirds of the custard cream. Cover with half the sliced strawberries. Place the second sponge layer on top and spread with the remaining custard cream and strawberries. Put on the top cake layer.
4. Using the remaining whipped cream, pipe eight large whirls of cream evenly round the top and decorate with strawberries. Pipe eight smaller whirls of cream in between the first and top with chocolate triangles.

**VARIATIONS:**
Strawberries may be replaced by any other soft fruit, or by 4–5 fresh peaches, sliced and dipped in Apricot Glaze (page 27). Frozen fruits may also be used, but remove excess juice before assembling and keep a few pieces of fruit almost frozen for the top decoration.
A sprinkling of Kirsch or Cointreau may be added to the sponge before assembling.
The cake may be baked in a well greased and lined angel cake tin, allowing about 45 minutes.

# CHOCOLATE RUM MERINGUE GATEAU

*Serves 8*
*Preparation time: 30–40 minutes,*
*    plus chilling*
*Cooking time: 2½–3¼ hours*
*Oven: 110°C, 225°F, Gas Mark ¼*

4 egg whites
150 g/6 oz light soft brown sugar,
    sifted
50 g/2 oz caster sugar

FILLING:
50 g/2 oz plain chocolate
1 recipe quantity ingredients for
    Confectioner's Custard (page
    27)
1 tablespoon rum

DECORATION:
150 ml/¼ pint double or whipping
    cream
1–2 tablespoons milk
40 g/1½ oz plain chocolate, grated
    or in curls (page 40)

The meringue can be made the day before, in which case store it in an airtight container.

1.  Draw a 20 cm/8 inch circle on each of two sheets of non-stick silicone paper and place on two baking sheets.
2.  Whisk the egg whites until very stiff. Mix the brown sugar with the caster sugar, then gradually whisk into the egg white a spoonful at a time, making sure the meringue is very stiff again before adding further sugar.
3.  Put the meringue into a piping bag fitted with a star vegetable nozzle and pipe a continuous coil to cover each of the circles, making one a fraction larger than the other. Use the remaining meringue to pipe about 12 small meringues on another baking sheet lined with non-stick silicone paper.
4.  Bake in a preheated oven, allowing

about 2 hours for the small meringues and 2½–3¼ hours for the rounds, or until dry and crisp and easy to peel off the paper. Reverse the sheets in the oven after 1 hour. Leave to cool.
5.  To make the filling, melt the chocolate in the milk used to make the confectioner's custard, then continue as the recipe states. Stir in the rum, cover with cling film or wet greaseproof paper and leave to cool.
6.  To assemble the gâteau, place the larger meringue round on a flat plate, spread the chocolate custard evenly over it and top with the second meringue round.
7.  Whip the cream and milk together until stiff, then spread over the top. Arrange the small meringues around the top edge so they just touch each other. Sprinkle the centre with the grated chocolate or curls.
8.  Chill for 10–15 minutes before serving, but do not assemble more than 45 minutes before required.

# PRALINE MERINGUE LAYER

*Serves 8*
*Preparation time: about 25 minutes,*
*plus chilling*
*Cooking time: 2½–3 hours*
*Oven: 110°C, 225°F, Gas Mark ¼*

4 egg whites
225 g/8 oz caster sugar

**PRALINE FILLING AND DECORATION:**
75 g/3 oz caster sugar
75 g/3 oz whole unblanched
  almonds
450 ml/¾ pint double or whipping
  cream
8 large strawberries, or 16 fresh
  raspberries or cherries
  or 8 fresh apricots, halved and
  stoned

The meringue and praline can both be made several days in advance if stored in airtight containers. Simply assemble when required.

1. Draw a rectangle 30 × 10 cm/12 × 4 inches on each of three sheets of non-stick silicone paper. Place on three baking sheets.
2. Whisk the egg whites until very stiff, then gradually whisk in the sugar a spoonful at a time, making sure the meringue is stiff again before adding further sugar.
3. Put the meringue into a piping bag fitted with a large star nozzle and pipe to cover the rectangles.
4. Bake in a preheated oven for 2½–3 hours, moving the meringues around in the oven after each hour, until dry and crisp and easy to peel off the paper. Leave to cool.

5. Meanwhile, make the praline for the filling. Put the sugar and almonds into a small heavy-based saucepan and heat gently until the sugar melts. Shake the saucepan to coat all the nuts with the sugar syrup, but do not stir. Cook gently until the sugar turns a good caramel colour, shaking the pan from time to time.
6. Spoon eight individual almonds on to one end of a well-greased sheet, making sure they are evenly coated in caramel. Quickly pour the remaining praline mixture on to the other end of the sheet and leave until cold.
7. Reserving the eight individual almonds, crush the sheet of praline using a rolling pin, pestle and mortar, small mouli cheese grater, liquidizer or food processor (but take care as it may well scratch the surface of the bowl).
8. Assemble the gâteau not more than 45 minutes before required. Whip the cream until stiff; put about one-third of it into a piping bag fitted with a large star nozzle. Fold the crushed praline into the remaining cream.
9. Place one meringue layer on a plate or board, spread with half the praline cream and cover with the second meringue layer. Spread over the rest of the praline cream and top with the third meringue layer.
10. Pipe whirls or a zig-zag pattern of cream along the top of the gâteau and decorate with the whole caramelled almonds and pieces of fresh fruit. Chill for 10–15 minutes before serving.

**Left: Praline meringue layer**
**Right: Chocolate rum meringue gâteau**

# ST SIMON'S GATEAU

*Serves 8*
*Preparation time: about 1 hour,*
  *plus chilling*
*Cooking time: about 1 hour*
*Oven: 160°C, 325°F, Gas Mark 3;*
  *220°C, 425°F, Gas Mark 7*

75 g/3 oz plain flour
50 g/2 oz butter
25 g/1 oz caster sugar
1½ recipe quantities Choux Paste
  (page 120)

FILLING:
600 ml/1 pint double or whipping
  cream
2–3 tablespoons milk
2 tablespoons Kirsch
1 fresh pineapple, peeled
2 tablespoons sifted icing sugar

CARAMEL:
225 g/8 oz granulated sugar
15 ml/¼ pint water

Do not assemble this gâteau too far in advance or the choux paste and shortbread will become soggy. The shortbread and choux buns may be made the day before required, in which case refresh the buns in a preheated oven (180°C/350°F, Gas Mark 4) for about 5 minutes. Allow to cool before filling and assembling.

1.  Sift the flour into a mixing bowl. Add the butter and sugar and rub together until the mixture resembles breadcrumbs. Press together to form a pliable dough. Roll out between two sheets of greaseproof paper to a round about 18 cm/7 inches in diameter. Place on a baking sheet and peel off the top sheet of paper. Prick all over and crimp the edges.
2.  Bake in a preheated oven for about 25 minutes or until lightly browned. Cool on the paper, marking into eight wedges as the shortbread becomes firm. Increase the oven temperature.
3.  Put the choux paste into a piping bag fitted with a 2 cm/¾ inch plain nozzle. Pipe the choux paste into walnut-sized buns on greased baking sheets, keeping them well apart.
4.  Bake in a preheated oven for about 20–25 minutes, or until well risen, golden brown and firm to the touch. Pierce each bun once to allow steam to escape, return

to the oven and bake for a further 2 minutes. Cool on a wire rack.
5.  Whip 300 ml/½ pint of the cream with the milk until stiff. Fill the buns with the whipped cream, reserving a little for the decoration.
6.  Whip the remaining cream with the Kirsch until stiff.
7.  Cut four equal slices from the centre of the pineapple and reserve. Chop the remainder of the pineapple roughly and fold through the Kirsch-flavoured cream with the icing sugar. Pile this mixture into the centre of the shortbread making a mound above it.
8.  Stick the choux buns all round the cream mound to cover it completely.
9.  Quarter the reserved slices of pineapple and arrange round the edge of the gâteau, attaching with stars of the remaining plain whipped cream.
10.  Finally make the caramel. Melt the sugar gently in the water in a heavy-based saucepan, then boil until caramel coloured. Cool until the caramel begins to thicken but not set, then drizzle quickly all over the gâteau. Leave to set, then chill for 30 minutes before serving.

# ICED MERINGUE GATEAU

*Serves 8–10*
*Preparation time: about 1¼ hours,*
*  plus freezing*
*Cooking time: 2½–3 hours*
*Oven: 180°C, 350°F, Gas Mark 4;*
*  110°C, 225°F, Gas Mark ¼*

2-egg Whisked Sponge Cake
  mixture (page 14)
2 egg whites
100 g/4 oz caster sugar

**BANANA ICE CREAM:**

1 egg
2 egg yolks
300 ml/½ pint milk, almost boiling
50 g/2 oz caster sugar
1½ teaspoons powdered gelatine
2 tablespoons water
175 ml/6 fl oz double or whipping
  cream
2 bananas, peeled
juice of ½ lemon

**DECORATION:**

150 ml/¼ pint double or whipping
  cream (optional)
1 banana, peeled and sliced
little lemon juice
1–2 kiwi fruit, peeled and sliced

This gâteau may be stored in the freezer
for up to a month. Allow to thaw for 1
hour.

1. Bake the cake mixture in a greased and
base-lined 20 cm/8 inch loose-based cake
tin in a preheated oven for 25–30 minutes
or until well risen and firm to the touch.
Turn on to a wire rack to cool. Reduce the
oven temperature.
2. Draw a 20 cm/8 inch circle on each of
two sheets of non-stick silicone paper and
place on two baking sheets.
3. Whisk the egg whites until very stiff,
then gradually whisk in the sugar, a
spoonful at a time, making sure the
meringue is stiff again before adding
further sugar. Pipe or spread the meringue
inside the circles on the paper.
4. Bake in a preheated oven for about 2–
2½ hours or until dry and crisp and easy to
peel off the paper; reverse the baking
sheets in the oven after 1 hour. Cool.
5. For the ice cream, whisk the egg and
egg yolks in a heatproof bowl. Add the
milk and sugar and place the bowl over a
pan of gently simmering water. Cook
gently until the custard is fairly thick,
stirring. Allow to cool until lukewarm.
6. Dissolve the gelatine in the water in a
heatproof bowl over hot water. Cool
slightly, then stir into the custard. Cool
completely.

7. Whip the cream to soft peaks and fold it
into the custard.
8. Mash the bananas with the lemon juice
and fold into the custard mixture. Cover
with foil and freeze for 1–2 hours or until
the edges are well frozen and the ice cream
is very thick.
9. Remove the ice cream from the freezer
and beat well until completely smooth.
10. Place the cold sponge layer back into
the well-oiled tin in which it was baked.
Spoon on half the ice cream and cover with
one of the meringue rounds. Cover with
the remaining ice cream and place the
second meringue round on top, pressing it
down evenly. Return to the freezer until
the ice cream is firm.
11. To serve, remove the gâteau carefully
from the cake tin and place it on a plate.
Decorate the top with a little whipped
cream, if using, slices of banana dipped in
lemon juice and slices of kiwi fruit. Leave
in the refrigerator for about 15 minutes
before serving.

**VARIATIONS:**

Bananas may be replaced with other fruits
such as raspberries, strawberries, apricots,
etc., provided they are well mashed or
puréed first. Allow 150–225 g/6–8 oz fruit.
A chocolate-flavoured sponge may be
used as an alternative.

# ORANGE & COCONUT LAYER CAKE

*Serves 8*
*Preparation time: about 25 minutes*

250–275 g/9–10 oz full fat soft cheese

2 tablespoons clear honey

1 tablespoon orange juice

25 g/1 oz desiccated coconut

grated rind of ½ orange

1 tablespoon caster sugar

1 rectangular orange Torten Sponge Cake (page 15)

50 g/2 oz desiccated coconut, toasted

2 medium oranges, peeled and sliced

1. Beat the cheese until light and fluffy, then beat in the honey and enough orange juice to give a soft spreading consistency.
2. Stir the coconut, orange rind and sugar into one-third of the cheese mixture.
3. Cut the cake in half lengthways and sandwich together with the orange cheese filling.
4. Use the remaining cheese mixture to mask the whole cake. Coat the sides evenly with the toasted coconut.
5. Arrange the orange slices in a line down the centre of the cake.

**VARIATION:**
Make a vanilla torten sponge cake, if preferred.

# CHOCOLATE ORANGE CHEESECAKE

*Serves 8–10*
*Preparation time: about 30 minutes,*
*    plus chilling*
*Cooking time: about 10 minutes*

40 g/1½ oz plain chocolate
40 g/1½ oz butter or margarine
175 g/6 oz digestive biscuits,
    crushed

FILLING:

225 g/8 oz full fat soft cheese
75 g/3 oz caster sugar
grated rind of 1 orange
4 tablespoons orange juice
15 g/½ oz powdered gelatine
2 tablespoons lemon juice
large can evaporated milk, chilled
    overnight

DECORATION:

150 ml/¼ pint double or whipping
    cream
1½–2 packets plain chocolate
    finger biscuits
jellied orange slices

1. Melt the chocolate and butter or margarine in a saucepan over a gentle heat. Stir in the crushed biscuits until evenly coated, then press over the bottom of a well-greased 19–20 cm/7½–8 inch loose-based round cake tin. Chill until set.
2. To make the filling, beat the cheese and sugar until soft and smooth. Gradually beat in the orange rind and juice.
3. Dissolve the gelatine in the lemon juice in a heatproof bowl over a pan of hot water. Cool, then mix evenly through the cheese mixture.

4. Whisk the evaporated milk until very thick and standing in soft peaks, then quickly fold through the cheese mixture. Pour into the tin over the biscuit base and chill until set – preferably overnight.
5. Remove the cheesecake from the tin and place it on a plate. Whip the cream until stiff and spread a thin layer all round the sides of the cheesecake. Stick the chocolate finger biscuits round the sides.
6. Decorate the top with whirls of whipped cream and complete with jellied orange slices.

# SMALL CAKES & PASTRIES

Here you'll find lots of ideas for small cakes and pastries to fit all types of tea tables, from picnics to birthday spreads. There are both impressive cakes, for the smarter tea table such as éclairs and truffle cakes, as well as tempting but more everyday cakes, such as brownie squares. Slab cakes are an easy way of producing a large number of small cakes because they are easier and quicker to ice than the individual cakes and can simply be cut to shapes and size as required. These sponge fancies, are ideal for fêtes and cake stalls.

But the fun cakes cannot be forgotten and although they are more time consuming, the effort is very worthwhile, for who can resist a hedgehog or marzipan-covered ladybird!

# SPONGE FANCIES

*Makes 22*
*Preparation time: about 1 hour*
*Cooking time: about 35 minutes*
*Oven: 180°C, 350°F, Gas Mark 4,*
*or 160°C, 325°F, Gas Mark 3*

3-egg Whisked Sponge Cake
  mixture (page 14) or 3-egg
  Quick Mix Cake mixture (page
  12)
225 g/8 oz Marzipan (page 22)
  (optional)
1 recipe quantity Apricot Glaze
  (page 27)
Glacé Icing, made with 550 g/
  1¼ lb icing sugar (page 20)
food colourings
cocoa powder
225 g/8 oz icing sugar, sifted

SUGGESTED DECORATIONS:
mimosa balls
crystallized violets
chocolate beans
orange and lemon jelly slices

If possible use a day old cake, which won't crumble so easily when cut. A layer of marzipan makes it easier to ice the cakes but is not essential.

1. Bake the cake mixture in a greased and lined 28 × 18 × 4 cm/11 × 7 × 1½ inch cake tin for about 35 minutes; using the higher oven temperature for the whisked sponge cake mixture. Cool on a wire rack.
2. Remove the paper and trim the cake edges.
3. If using marzipan, roll it out to fit the top of the cake. Brush the top of the cake with apricot glaze and invert the cake on to the marzipan. Trim the edges and reserve the marzipan trimmings.
4. Cut the cake to give six rounds, six triangles, six bars and four squares. To do this cut six 5 cm/2 inch rounds in two rows at one end of the cake. Mark the remaining cake along the length into three sections; one 5 cm/2 inches wide, the centre section 6 cm/2½ inches wide, and the third section 4 cm/1½ inches wide. Cut three 5 cm/2 inch squares from the first section and cut diagonally into six triangles. Cut the central section into six 2.5 cm/1 inch bars, and the third section into four squares.
5. Carefully separate the shapes and stand with the marzipan uppermost.
6. Knead the marzipan trimmings to make small shapes such as rounds, triangles and rolls. Place on some of the cakes.

7. Divide the icing in half then stand the two bowls in saucepans of hot water, but off the heat.
8. Place one small cake of each shape on a wire rack and carefully coat the top and sides with icing from one bowl. When the icing stops dripping, trim off the edges. Leave to set.
9. Tint the remaining icing in that bowl pink, adding food colouring from the tip of a skewer. Use the pink icing to coat four more cakes, one of each shape.
10. Add a few drops of blue or mauve colouring to the remaining pink icing in the bowl to give a mauve colour and use to coat three more cakes of different shapes.
11. Tint the other bowl of white icing yellow and use to coat three cakes. Halve the remaining yellow icing and tint one part green or orange and the other part with sifted cocoa powder to give a rich brown. Use these to coat four cakes in each colour. Leave until all the cakes are set.
12. Make up the icing sugar to a thick glacé icing of piping consistency (adding more icing sugar if necessary). Put half of this into two greaseproof paper icing bags (see page 29), one fitted with a plain writing nozzle and the other with a fine star nozzle. Decorate some of the coloured cakes with zig-zag or straight lines, and borders or lines of stars or shells. Complete with mimosa balls, crystallized violets, chocolate beans and jellied slices.
13. Tint the bowl of remaining icing a different colour (or colours) or darker shade to tone with the cakes and use to decorate the remaining cakes in the same way. Leave to set. Serve in paper cake cases, if preferred.

**VARIATION:**
The cakes may be iced with Butter Cream (page 26). Make up 1 recipe quantity and divide it into three small bowls. Tint one portion green or pink with food colouring, the second pale brown with about 1 tablespoon of coffee essence, and the third dark brown with 1–2 tablespoons sifted cocoa powder. Brush the sides of the small cakes with apricot glaze but don't coat them with marzipan. Roll in 175–225 g/6–8 oz chopped toasted almonds or walnuts to coat the sides evenly. Spread a layer of butter cream over the top of each cake and decorate with piped shells, stars or a border of a contrasting butter cream, using a greaseproof paper icing bag fitted with a medium star nozzle. Complete the decoration with pieces of glacé cherry, pistachio nuts, grated chocolate, toasted almonds or walnuts.

# BROWNIES

*Makes 16*
*Preparation time: 10 minutes*
*Cooking time: 35–40 minutes*
*Oven: 180°C, 350°F, Gas Mark 4*

50 g/2 oz plain chocolate, broken into pieces, or chocolate dots
65 g/2½ oz butter or margarine
150 g/6 oz caster sugar
½ teaspoon vanilla essence
65 g/2½ oz self-raising flour
large pinch of salt
50 g/2 oz walnuts, chopped
2 eggs, beaten
little icing sugar (optional)

These chewy chocolate squares with a crisp crumbly top are a great American favourite. Brownies freeze well for up to 2 months; wrap in foil and cut when thawed.

1. Put the chocolate and butter or margarine into a heatproof bowl over a saucepan of gently simmering water. Heat until melted, stirring frequently.
2. Remove from the heat and beat in the caster sugar and vanilla essence.
3. Sift the flour and salt into a bowl and stir in the walnuts.
4. Add the eggs and chocolate mixture to the flour and beat until well combined.

5. Pour into a greased and floured shallow 20 cm/8 inch square tin and bake in a preheated oven for 35–40 minutes or until well risen and just beginning to shrink away from the sides of the tin.
6. Cool in the tin, then cut into 16 squares. Dredge with icing sugar before serving, if using. Store in an airtight container.

# NUTTY MERINGUES

*Makes 10*
*Preparation time: about 15 minutes*
*Cooking time: about 30 minutes*
*Oven: 150°C, 300°F, Gas Mark 2*

2 egg whites (sizes 1, 2)
150 g/5 oz icing sugar, sifted
50 g/2 oz hazelnuts or almonds, toasted and finely chopped

1. Put the egg whites and sugar into a heatproof bowl over a saucepan of gently simmering water and whisk until the mixture thickens and stands in stiff peaks.
2. Remove from the heat and beat in the hazelnuts or almonds.
3. Spoon the mixture into rounds about 5–6 cm/2–2½ inches in diameter on baking sheets lined with non-stick silicone paper or rice paper.

4. Bake in a preheated oven for about 30 minutes or until pale cream in colour and easily removed from the sheets. Leave to cool, then store in an airtight container.
5. Serve plain or topped with a whirl of whipped cream and a piece of soft fruit, a hazelnut, or Chocolate Curls (page 40). Alternatively, drizzle with melted chocolate.

# ALMOND TARTS

*Makes 14–16*
*Preparation time: 20 minutes*
*Cooking time: 15–20 minutes*
*Oven: 200°C, 400°F, Gas Mark 6*

100 g/4 oz plain flour
pinch of salt
25 g/1 oz butter or margarine
25 g/1 oz lard

FILLING:
raspberry or blackcurrant jam
50 g/2 oz butter or margarine
50 g/2 oz caster sugar
1 egg (sizes 1, 2), beaten
few drops of almond essence
40 g/1½ oz self-raising flour
15 g/½ oz ground almonds
25 g/1 oz flaked almonds
icing sugar

1. Sift the flour and salt into a bowl and rub in the butter or margarine and lard until the mixture resembles fine breadcrumbs. Add sufficient cold water to mix to a pliable dough.
2. Roll out the dough on a floured surface and cut into 14–16 rounds using a 7.5 cm/3 inch fluted cutter. Use to line 14–16 greased or dampened patty tins.
3. Spread a little jam in the bottom of each tart case.
4. Cream the butter or margarine and caster sugar together until fluffy and pale in colour. Beat in the egg followed by the almond essence.
5. Sift the flour, mix with the ground almonds and fold into the creamed mixture.

6. Divide the filling between the tart cases and level the tops. Sprinkle each with a few flaked almonds.
7. Bake in a preheated oven for 15–20 minutes or until the tarts are well risen and golden brown.
8. Cool on a wire rack. Dredge lightly with sifted icing sugar before serving.

**Clockwise from the top: Brownies; Nutty meringues; Almond tarts**

# BUTTERFLIES

*Makes 8*
*Preparation time: about 20 minutes*
*Cooking time: 10–12 minutes*
*Oven: 220°C, 425°F, Gas Mark 7*

225 g/8 oz puff pastry, thawed if
  frozen
caster sugar
ground cinnamon
icing sugar
½ recipe quantity Glacé Icing
  (page 20)
food colouring
8 coloured chocolate sweets or
  chocolate beans
few strips of candied angelica

1. Roll out the dough on a floured surface and trim to a 30 cm/12 inch square. Dredge well with caster sugar, then sprinkle lightly with ground cinnamon.
2. Mark a faint line down the centre of the square. Roll up two opposite sides of the square loosely, almost to this centre line.
3. Cut across the rolls into 16 equal slices. Place these, cut sides down, in pairs on a greased baking sheet, placing the long edges together to give a butterfly shape.
4. Bake in a preheated oven for 10–12 minutes or until puffy and golden brown. The 'wings' should open out during baking. Cool on a wire rack.

5. Lightly dredge the butterfly wings with sifted icing sugar.
6. Make up the glacé icing, keeping it very thick. Tint it pink, yellow, green or orange. Place in a greaseproof paper icing bag (see page 29) without a nozzle.
7. Cut off the tip of the icing bag and pipe a thick line backwards and forwards between the 'wings' to give a 'body'. Position a sweet for the head and two narrow strips of angelica to represent antennae. Leave to set.

# MERINGUE MICE

*Makes 12*
*Preparation time: 15 minutes*
*Cooking time: 2 hours*
*Oven: 110°C, 225°F, Gas Mark ¼*

2 egg whites (sizes 1, 2)
100 g/4 oz caster or light soft
    brown sugar, sifted
few pink coloured or silver balls
liquorice or strawberry flavoured
    'bootlaces' or 'coils'

These are fun for a children's party. For white meringues caster sugar must be used, but the flavour of brown sugar makes delicious meringues. For pink mice, use caster sugar and add a few drops of pink food colouring. The ears can also be made by adding small pieces of Marzipan (page 22).

1. Whisk the egg whites until very stiff and dry, and standing in peaks.
2. Gradually whisk in the sugar, a spoonful at a time, making sure the meringue is stiff again before adding further sugar.

3. Using two tablespoons, mould 'mouse' shapes of meringue on baking sheets lined with non-stick silicone paper, smoothing with a palette knife as necessary.
4. Put two coloured or silver balls on the 'mice' for eyes and one for a nose. Tiny points can be pulled up in the meringue for ears.
5. Bake in a preheated oven for about 2 hours or until the meringues are set and easily removed from the paper. Reverse the baking sheets in the oven after 1 hour. Cool completely on the baking sheets.
6. Cut the liquorice into narrow strips about 7.5 cm/3 inches long. Make a small hole in the meringue mice with a skewer and position the liquorice to give the mice long tails.

**VARIATIONS:**
The meringue may be piped into whirls, bun shapes, fingers or twisted fingers, stars, shells, etc., using a piping bag fitted with a plain or star vegetable nozzle. Bake as above. Serve plain or sandwiched together in pairs with whipped cream.
*For coffee meringues:* whisk in 1 teaspoon instant coffee powder with the sugar.
*For chocolate meringues:* whisk in 1½ teaspoons sifted cocoa powder.

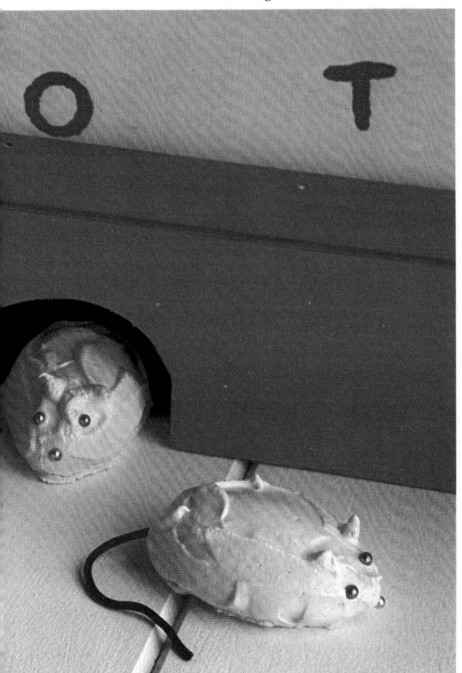

# CHOCOLATE ECLAIRS

*Makes 20–24*
*Preparation time: 20 minutes*
*Cooking time: 20–25 minutes*
*Oven: 220°C, 425°F, Gas Mark 7*

150 ml/¼ pint double or whipping cream or 1 recipe quantity Confectioner's Custard (page 27)

**CHOUX PASTE:**
50 g/2 oz butter or margarine
150 ml/¼ pint water
65 g/2½ oz plain flour
pinch of salt
2 eggs (sizes 1, 2), beaten

**TOPPING:**
100 g/4 oz plain or milk chocolate
25 g/1 oz butter

For round éclairs simply pipe the choux paste into buns about the size of a large walnut.

1. To make the choux paste, melt the butter or margarine in the water in a saucepan, then bring to the boil. Remove from the heat.
2. Sift the flour and salt together and tip all at once into the pan. Beat with a wooden spoon to give a smooth paste which forms into a ball.
3. Spread out the paste over the bottom of the pan and leave to cool for several minutes.
4. Gradually beat in the eggs until the mixture is smooth and glossy and gives a piping consistency. A hand-held electric mixer is ideal for this task.
5. Put the choux paste into a piping bag fitted with a plain 1 cm/½ inch nozzle. Pipe the paste into straight lines about 6 cm/2½ inches long, spaced well apart, on greased baking sheets. Cut the ends of the paste from the nozzle with a knife.

6. Bake in a preheated oven for 20–25 minutes or until well risen, firm and a pale golden brown.
7. Make a slit in the side of each éclair to allow the steam to escape and return to the oven to dry out for a few minutes.
8. Transfer to a wire rack to cool.
9. If using cream to fill the éclairs, whip it until stiff. Slit each éclair in half carefully and fill with the cream or confectioner's custard.
10. Melt the chocolate in a heatproof bowl over hot water, then stir in the butter until melted. Remove from the heat and cool until beginning to thicken.
11. Dip the top of each éclair into the topping or spread with a palette knife. Leave to set.

**VARIATION:**
Ice the éclairs with chocolate or coffee Glacé Icing (page 20).

# CREAM SLICES

*Makes 6*
*Preparation time: 20–30 minutes*
*Cooking time: 15–20 minutes*
*Oven: 230°C, 450°F, Gas Mark 8*

200–225 g/7–8 oz puff or flaky pastry, thawed if frozen
1 recipe quantity Glacé Icing (page 20)
pink food colouring
6–8 tablespoons raspberry jam or bramble jelly
150 ml/¼ pint double or whipping cream

1. Roll out the dough thinly and trim to a rectangle 30 × 25 cm/12 × 10 inches. Cut in half lengthways and then into 12 strips, 13 × 5 cm/5 × 2 inches.
2. Place the dough strips on lightly greased or dampened baking sheets. Bake in a preheated oven for 15–20 minutes or until well risen and golden brown. Cool on a wire rack.
3. Put 1 tablespoon of the glacé icing in a small bowl and tint it a deep pink with food colouring. Put into a greaseproof paper icing bag (see page 29).

4. Spread the white glacé icing over the tops of the six best pastry strips. Cut the tip off the paper icing bag and quickly pipe lines across the white icing at 1 cm/½ inch intervals. Immediately draw a skewer down the length of the strip at 1 cm/½ inch intervals, first from one end and then the other to make feathering. Leave to set.
5. Spread the remaining strips of pastry with the jam. Whip the cream until stiff and spread over the jam.
6. Complete by placing the iced strips of pastry on top. Chill before serving.

# LEMON MERINGUE BARS

*Makes 12–14*
*Preparation time: 15–20 minutes*
*Cooking time: about 45 minutes*
*Oven: 160°C, 325°F, Gas Mark 3*

100 g/4 oz butter or margarine
100 g/4 oz caster sugar
3 eggs, separated
grated rind of 1 large lemon
2 tablespoons lemon juice
200 g/8 oz self-raising flour, sifted
50 g/2 oz walnuts, chopped
150 g/6 oz icing sugar, sifted

1. Cream the butter or margarine and caster sugar together until fluffy and pale in colour. Beat in the egg yolks, lemon rind and juice.
2. Gradually beat in the flour to give a fairly stiff consistency.
3. Press evenly into a shallow 28 × 18 cm/11 × 7 inch tin lined with non-stick silicone paper. Sprinkle over the walnuts.
4. Whisk the egg whites until very stiff, then gradually whisk in the icing sugar, reserving 1 tablespoon.
5. Spread the meringue evenly over the walnuts, pulling it up into peaks. Sprinkle with the reserved icing sugar.

6. Bake in a preheated oven for about 45 minutes or until a pale brown.
7. Cool in the tin, then carefully cut into bars.

**VARIATIONS:**
Orange or grapefruit rind and juice may be used in place of lemon.
Hazelnuts or toasted almonds may be substituted for the walnuts.

**Clockwise from the front: Lemon meringue bars; Chocolate éclairs; Cream slices**

# BRANDY SNAPS

*Makes 12–16*
*Preparation time: 20 minutes*
*Cooking time: about 40 minutes*
*Oven: 160°C, 325°F, Gas Mark 3*

50 g/2 oz butter or margarine
50 g/2 oz caster sugar
50 g/2 oz golden syrup
50 g/2 oz plain flour
¼ teaspoon ground ginger

FILLING (optional):
whipped cream and a few pieces
  of stem or crystallized ginger, or
  brandy Butter Cream (page 26)

These can be made into traditional 'snaps', which are rolled around greased wooden spoon handles, or 'cornets' using greased cream horn tins. Size can vary to suit the occasion. If possible use three baking sheets because the brandy snaps need to be baked and shaped in batches. Each batch should be baked on a cool baking sheet.

1. Melt the butter or margarine in a saucepan with the sugar and syrup. Remove from the heat.
2. Sift the flour and ginger and beat into the melted mixture.
3. Put four or five teaspoons of the mixture on to baking sheets lined with non-stick silicone paper, spacing well apart. For mini brandy snaps use coffee spoonfuls of the mixture.

4. Bake in a preheated oven for about 10 minutes or until an even golden brown.
5. Allow to cool for 1–2 minutes until slightly firm, then carefully ease off the baking sheet one at a time with the help of a palette knife. Immediately wind round a greased wooden spoon handle or cream horn tin.
6. If the wafers become too hard and brittle to wind, return briefly to the oven to soften up again.
7. Cool on a wire rack until firm, then slide off the handles or tins.
8. Cook and shape the remaining mixture similarly.
9. Store in an airtight container until required.
10. Serve plain or fill with whipped cream and a piece of ginger, or brandy-flavoured butter cream just before serving.

# TRUFFLE CAKES

*Makes 8*
*Preparation time: 25 minutes,*
*plus chilling*
*Cooking time: about 5 minutes*

225 g/8 oz plain chocolate, broken
 into pieces
50 g/2 oz dry cake crumbs
50 g/2 oz Nice, digestive or ginger
 biscuits, crushed
25 g/1 oz glacé cherries, chopped
2 tablespoons apricot jam
1 tablespoon coffee essence or
 strong black coffee

DECORATION:
150 ml/¼ pint double or whipping
 cream or 1 recipe quantity
 vanilla, coffee, or brandy Butter
 Cream (page 26)
4 glacé cherries, halved
8 Chocolate Leaves (page 41)

1. Melt the chocolate in a heatproof bowl over hot water.
2. Using a pastry brush, coat the insides of eight paper cake cases with half the melted chocolate. Chill until set, then add a second layer of chocolate. Chill for several hours or overnight until very firm.
3. Mix together the cake and biscuit crumbs. Add the cherries and bind together with the jam and coffee essence or coffee.
4. Carefully peel the paper from the chocolate cases and arrange them on a plate. Fill with the cake mixture.
5. If using cream to decorate, whip it until stiff. Pipe a whirl of cream or butter cream on top of the filling. Complete with half a glacé cherry and a chocolate leaf.

# DALEKS

*Makes 8*
*Preparation time: 20 minutes*
*Cooking time: about 25 minutes*
*Oven: 160°C, 325°F, Gas Mark 3*

2-egg vanilla or coffee Quick Mix
  Cake mixture (page 12)
1 recipe quantity Butter Cream
  (page 26)
pink and green food colouring
16 chocolate matchsticks
8 round marshmallows (pink and
  white)
coloured chocolate sweets

1.  Divide the cake mixture between eight well-greased and floured dariole moulds, filling each almost three-quarters full. Bake in a preheated oven for about 25 minutes or until well risen and firm to the touch.
2.  Cool for a few minutes in the tins, then trim off the tops of the cakes evenly and turn out carefully. Leave the cakes to cool on a wire rack.
3.  Divide the butter cream in half. Colour one portion pink and the other green.
4.  Mask the cakes with the butter cream, four pink and four green. Put the remaining butter cream into piping bags fitted with medium star nozzles.
5.  Pipe a 'collar' of matching butter cream around the top of each dalek and put two

chocolate matchsticks in position for antennae.
6.  Place a marshmallow on top of each dalek and attach a sweet on the top with butter cream.
7.  Stick various coloured sweets all over the 'bodies' of the daleks and leave to set.

# HAPPY HEDGEHOGS

*Makes 8*
*Preparation time: 20 minutes*
*Cooking time: 35–40 minutes*
*Oven: 160°C, 325°F, Gas Mark 3*

3-egg chocolate or coffee Quick
  Mix Cake mixture (page 12)
1 recipe quantity chocolate Butter
  Cream (page 26)
plain chocolate vermicelli
few silver balls
8 chocolate buttons or beans

1.  Bake the cake mixture in a greased greaseproof paper-lined 28 × 18 × 4 cm/ 11 × 7 × 1½ inch tin in a preheated oven for 35–40 minutes or until well risen and firm to the touch. Turn out and cool on a wire rack.
2.  When cold, cut the cake into eight 6 cm/ 2½ inch rounds.
3.  Mask each piece of cake with butter cream, giving it a rounded shape and pulling the butter cream into peaks all over except at one end which should be smooth for the head.

4.  Apart from the head sprinkle the hedgehogs all over with chocolate vermicelli.
5.  Add silver (or coloured) balls for eyes and a chocolate button or bean for a nose. Leave to set.

# LADYBIRDS

*Makes about 18*
*Preparation time: 30 minutes*
*Cooking time: 15–20 minutes*
*Oven: 160°C, 325°F, Gas Mark 3*

2-egg vanilla or chocolate Quick
   Mix Cake mixture (page 12)
225–350 g/8–12 oz marzipan
red food colouring
1 recipe quantity Apricot Glaze
   (page 27)
50 g/2 oz chocolate, melted
9 chocolate-coated peppermint
   cream sweets, halved
chocolate dots

1. Divide the cake mixture between about 18 paper cake cases or greased and floured patty tins. Bake in a preheated oven for 15–20 minutes or until well risen and firm to the touch. Turn out and allow to cool on a wire rack. If necessary, trim the cakes so they stand evenly.
2. Knead the marzipan until pliable, then gradually knead in food colouring to give a good even red colour. The amount of marzipan necessary depends on the thickness of coating required.
3. Roll out the marzipan thinly between two sheets of polythene and cut into 8 cm/ 3¼ inch rounds. Roll the trimmings to make a total of about 18 rounds.
4. Brush the marzipan rounds with apricot glaze and press one evenly over each cake.
5. Use a little melted chocolate to attach half a peppermint cream to the marzipan on each cake for a head. Paint a line of chocolate down the centre back of each ladybird. Use chocolate to stick three or four chocolate dots to the body.
6. Mark two chocolate 'eyes' with the paint brush and leave to set.

# INDEX

# USEFUL ADDRESSES

The following are specialist shops for personal shoppers and mail order. They can supply many of the items for cake decorating.

**Baker Smith (Cake Decorators) Ltd**
The School of Cake Decorating
65 The Street
Tongham
Farnham
Surrey GU10 1DE
Tel: Runfold (025 18) 2984

**Cookcraft Club Ltd** (*mail order only*)
20 Canterbury Road,
Herne Bay
Kent
Tel: Herne Bay (022 73) 3049

**Cakecraft Studio** (*personal shoppers only*)
same address as
Cookcraft Club Ltd (above)
open Mon, Wed, Sat 10–4

**F. & P. Catering Services Ltd**
43–45 Hoe Street
Walthamstow
London E17
Tel: (01) 520 0893/0525

**Homebakers Supplies**
157–159 High Street
Wolstanton
Newcastle
Staffs ST5 0EJ
Tel: Wolstanton (0782) 614119

**Mary Ford Cake Artistry Centre**
28–30 Southbourne Grove
Southbourne
Bournemouth
Dorset BH6 3RA
Tel: Bournemouth (0202) 426466/422653

**Woodnutt's**
97 Church Road
Hove
Brighton
Sussex
Tel: Brighton (0273) 738840

**Cakecraft Artistry & Sundries**
(*mail order only*)
54 Hazelwick Road
Three Bridges
Crawley
Sussex
Tel: Crawley (0293) 20875

## ACKNOWLEDGEMENTS

**Photography: Peter Myers**
**Photographic styling: Antonia Gaunt, Penny Markham and Alison Williams**
**Preparation of food for photography: Rosemary Wadey**

The publishers would also like to thank E.F. Langdale, Ltd., for their assistance: Fanciful Winnie the Pooh characters, pages 48 and 89, © Walt Disney Productions. Text by A.A. Milne (page 89), copyright under the Berne Convention.